raising
happy
kids

A message from Michael Grose, author of *Raising Happy Kids*.

To subscribe to Michael's free newsletter *Happy Kids* send an e-mail to parents-request@listhost.net and type "subscribe" (without the quotation marks) in the body of the message.

Test your knowledge about kids by taking this quiz on www.parentingideas.com.au

Phone: (03) 5983 1798.

E-mail mgrose@pac.com.au.

MICHAEL GROSE

raising
happy
kids

A guide to happy parenting

HarperCollins*Publishers*

HarperCollins*Publishers*

First published in Australia in 1999
by HarperCollins*Publishers* Pty Limited
ACN 009 913 517
A member of the HarperCollins*Publishers* (Australia) Pty Limited Group
http://www.harpercollins.com.au

HarperCollins*Publishers*
25 Ryde Road, Pymble, Sydney NSW 2073, Australia
31 View Road, Glenfield, Auckland 10, New Zealand

The National Library of Australia Cataloguing-in-Publication data:

Grose, Michael, 1955- .
  Raising happy kids.
  ISBN 0 7322 5987 8.
  1. Parenting. 2. Parent and child. 3. Child psychology.
  I. Title.
649.1

Printed in Australia by Griffin Press Pty Ltd on 80gsm Ensobelle.

9 8 7 6 5 4 3 2 1
02 01 00 99

CONTENTS

INTRODUCTION

Great things happen in life.

MALCOLM BLIGHT,
COACH OF ADELAIDE FOOTBALL CLUB,
1997-98 BACK-TO-BACK AFL PREMIERS
26 SEPTEMBER 1998

The Chinese have a saying 'May you live in interesting times.' Raising kids as we enter the new century is a confusing, anxious experience for many parents. In fact, confusion about how best to raise children and anxiety about their safety and future are characteristics that galvanise Australian parents.

Many parents feel powerless in their attempts to raise their children. Too many outside influences, too much change, too much choice and too little time are enemies of today's parents. But parents do matter in the lives of kids. Many parents busily divest their responsibilities to others to raise and teach their children. This is not through selfishness but for a variety of reasons including lack of time and, significantly, a lack of faith in their abilities to raise and teach their children.

Today's parents are a very anxious group. They are uncertain about their children's futures and extremely concerned about current issues such as drugs and alcohol abuse. For the first time in decades our young are not assured of employment or, indeed, a better economic future than their parents. Perhaps this explains the current obsession many parents have with providing their children with an early start in life. It seems that everything starts young these days. Kids as young as three take computer lessons, dance lessons or music lessons.

Raising children has become corporatised. In many ways children are seen as products and problems rather than resources. We now have a burgeoning before-and-after school industry providing kids with a range of activities. Parents of young children are keen to get their children off to a flying start, while many parents of older school-aged children will go to great lengths to give their kids the winning edge. With the pressure to succeed beginning from an early age, we risk robbing children of the sweet essence of childhood where they can develop slowly and 'muck around'. I am not suggesting that children don't take dance lessons, attend Brownies or do other extra-curricular activities, but there is a concern about the number of activities that they do. When parents are reduced to little more than taxi-driver status taking children from one activity to another, surely it is time to sit back and review their role and place in children's lives.

The child improvement industry is evidence of parents looking outwards rather than at themselves to provide children with a start to life. I strongly believe that parents underestimate the part they play in the lives and the development of children. It is the values, attitudes and strengths that they pass on to children that make an enduring difference, not the skills they may pick up from a class or an interest that they have cultivated.

There is an intense feeling of pressure among Australian parents not to muck up. A young man who came to one of my parenting seminars best sums up this anxiety. His partner was pregnant with their first child and he was asking questions about suitable television-viewing habits for children and other issues that he would meet further down the track as a father. When I suggested that he relax a little and just let things happen, he replied, 'I have only one chance as a parent and I want to do it right.' That's a lot of pressure to place on yourself!

Make no mistake, good parenting counts; it makes a huge difference. The tennis lessons, the influence of media and music on kids, the influence of peers from an increasingly younger age are side issues. Parents always have been, and always will be, the main event in the lives of children and young people. It is time to regain some parental self-esteem and have faith in our ability to influence our children in the important aspects of their lives. Parents also need to be supported by healthy, caring communities in their task of raising children from birth to adulthood.

Much of the confusion parents experience can be linked to the rapid changes in technology. Few things remain the same these days. Today's piece of hardware is tomorrow's rubbish; the computer that I am working on now will be replaced by a newer, better model by the time you read these words. Change is a constant. Along with advances in technology and communication systems, we are also seeing changes in ideas and values. Today everything is questioned. As parents we constantly look back to our own experiences of being parented for clues, but increasingly these experiences are irrelevant. More than ever parents are looking outwards for help and advice.

According to Richard Neville (Melbourne *Age*, 24 September 1998):

> *Children are passing from the chrysalis of the high chair to fully fledged teenagerdom at the speed of light transmitted by fibre optic. Time, space and values are blurring. Fast disappearing along with the concept of childhood are secrets, privacy, guilt, truth and a sense of core values.*

Kids today are more streetwise than we were and grow up faster than the previous generation. It is increasingly difficult to protect children or closet them from adult concepts. The death of rock star Michael Hutchence resulted in children as young as seven or eight in one school discussing his life and untimely demise and speculating about the reasons for him taking his own life. His demise, like that of Princess Diana, received saturation coverage in all forms of the media with little information left to one's imagination. A recent Hollywood remake of the movie *The Parent Trap* gives some idea of how childhood is rapidly shrinking. The original movie filmed in 1961 featured fourteen-year-old twins as the main characters who tried to reunite their divorced parents. In the 1998 remake, the producers took three years off the main characters' ages. Producer Nancy Meyers justified this decision, saying, 'We figured that for practical purposes an 11 year old these days would be equivalent to a 14-year-old in

1961. These days, 14-year-olds are probably too absorbed by their own romantic lives to worry about those of their parents and, besides, we didn't want to have to deal with piercings and tattoos that go with that age group.' Childhood was once a secret garden; now there are few fences to keep adulthood at bay.

In a physical sense, childhood is shrinking as children are reaching puberty earlier each decade. The World Health Organization states that children in westernised countries begin puberty three months earlier every decade. It is no coincidence that teachers in primary schools across the country report prepubescent behaviour that was once only found in secondary schools. Parents have a shrinking window of opportunity in which they can really influence their children; blink and they have grown up before you know it.

An increasing number of Australian families live life in a very fast lane indeed. The increase of mothers into the work force and the trend for those with jobs to put in longer hours means that time has now become a luxury item. The rapid rise in the home-help industry, which includes everything from lawn mowing to house cleaning and grocery shopping, is indicative of our attempts to purchase some free time. Family time competes with other priorities as parents juggle competing demands and parenting becomes the 'second shift'.

Lack of time undoubtedly has an impact on the way children are raised. One mother, at the end of a parenting program that I conducted, remarked that she liked the ideas that I presented but she didn't have time to implement them. She basically wanted compliance from her children and she stated that her main difficulties were getting her children out the door and into child care with a minimum of fuss. Like many parents I have worked with, she wanted a quick fix for any difficulties she encountered. Child management was her main concern. It is noteworthy that the concept of patience is not a term used in parenting much these days as we look for quick solutions to sometimes long-term problems.

Parenting – something that was passed down from one generation to the next – has now almost become a profession as theories abound about the best way of raising kids. More and more people are looking out rather than within to find the solutions to some of their parenting dilemmas. We also tend to look outwards for answers when difficulties emerge or even to experts for advice in many areas of our lives. The proliferation of lifestyle programs on television is evidence of our submission to the expert to provide us with the answers. Once we would have sought advice from our neighbour about when to plant tomatoes, or where the fish are biting. Now we are more likely to listen to advice given by an expert on television or radio.

Another disturbing trend is the constant malignment of adolescents in the media. We are constantly reminded of adolescent problems, particularly drug and alcohol problems and suicide. While it would be foolish to deny that we have youth problems that need addressing, it is easy to forget that the majority of adolescents grow into fully functioning adults who lead satisfying lives. The focus in the media on negative aspects of adolescence reinforces the anxiety that many parents have about raising children.

Popular opinion implies that parenting, particularly of adolescents, is something to be endured rather than enjoyed. As my children move into adolescence I have been heartened by many parents who have assured me that raising their teenagers was a positive, albeit testing, experience for them. Raising adolescents was, in fact, a growth experience for them.

Many parents look at parenting through a management perspective, which is a limited way of viewing raising kids. Much of what passes as effective parenting focuses on management techniques and, to a lesser extent, on compliance and decision-making within families. The language of the boardroom and the battleground are common as parents use terms such as 'coping', 'surviving', 'tactics' and 'strategies' when referring to their children.

The autocratic style of management has been replaced by a democratic or authoritative approach. The push for promoting children's self-esteem is also a product of the parents-as-managers approach.

This is not a book about child management but a book about leadership. It is a positive book that explores how we as parents, teachers and community members can help kids become healthy, functioning adults ready to meet challenges and able to thrive as we enter the twenty-first century. In many ways it is a reclaiming of some of the child-rearing ways that we have lost. It is not a call for the past; rather, it is a reworking of the successful ways that have been used to raise kids to be resilient and optimistic about the future.

This book is for parents, teachers, professionals and anyone who has an interest in children. They are crying out for good leadership from the significant adults in their lives. This book will help you to become an effective leader, not just of children but of those around you. Our job as parents and teachers is to provide children with a foundation of skills and values and the space and opportunities to grow as individuals as they get older.

Part 1 focuses on leadership – what leadership is about and how it differs from management. It looks at how parents can create harmonious and challenging environments for children and how they can discipline their children as leaders rather than managers.

Part 2 looks at the competencies, skills and values that we can help to provide for children and young people. This section draws together some important work by professionals and authors in the field. In particular, it draws from the work of Martin Seligman, who teaches us how to promote a sense of optimism in children that remains for life. It implements many of the ideas of Bonnie Benard and others in the important field of resiliency promotion.

This part also presents some of the work of John Gottman, who encourages adults to promote a sense of emotional literacy in their children so that they can become more aware of their own emotional lives and those of children and young people. Attending to the hidden world of emotions is surely one skill that we must give our boys, who typically find it difficult dealing with their feelings.

This part also outlines some of the values and strengths that parents and teachers should promote in children.

Part 3 explores the role of schools and communities in supporting families and children. Using the wonderful ideas from the resilience movement, it looks at how we can provide for real youth development in a way that builds on their strengths, rather than weaknesses, and that forms connections and enables them to contribute to the lives of others.

Part 1

POSITIVE FAMILY LEADERSHIP

In the second half of the twentieth century, two phenomena occurred that have placed young people at risk.

The first is that we reduced the amount of meaningful contact that children have with adults over the course of the century. For thousands of years, children and young people have spent a significant amount of time in the company of adults in their immediate family, their wider family and their community. They have learned about themselves and their world through constant interaction with adults. The Industrial Revolution in the mid-nineteenth century brought significant changes for children and families. During this time families left rural communities and went to cities, and adults left their homes and farms to work in factories and offices. The continued urbanisation of the twentieth century and, in Australia, the high level of mobility of people caused partly by the tyranny of distance, led to the peculiar institution known as the nuclear family. The dual-income family is now the norm as increasingly both parents in two-parent families work.

And they are working longer hours, with the number of Australians working fifty hours or more a week doubling since 1984. The average family of the 1930s spent three or four hours interacting with each other, usually around the kitchen table, which was the centre of the house. Various studies in both Australia and the USA indicate that the average family interacts with each other in a meaningful way (with the television off) for about twelve minutes a day. Parents have less time to spend with their children than ever and increasingly use paid and community assistance for many of the child-rearing practices that their parents and grandparents did themselves.

While parents and communities have been distancing themselves from the lives of children, the peer group has been playing an increasingly influential role in child-raising. American researcher and leader in the field of family and child development E. Timothy Burns claims that children spend as much time interacting with their peers free from adult supervision in one day as their great-grandparents did in a month. Away from the influence and teaching of positive adult role models, kids look to each other and media personalities for cues about how to act, think, behave and live. The most extreme peer group is the teenage gang that serves as a surrogate family and community for many young people.

Peer influence is not negative in itself. Melbourne's Professor Michael Carr-Gregg successfully harnessed the positive power of the peer group when he began CANTEEN, a peer support group for teenage cancer patients. But peers are not adults. Young people are staying at school longer, apprenticeships have all but disappeared and few formal mentoring systems operate between adults and young people for the passing down of skills, information, values and ideas that lay the pathway to adulthood.

Moving into adolescence means moving away from parents, but it shouldn't mean moving away from adults. Communities are not playing their part in raising the next generation.

The second phenomenon is the proliferation of the media and its influence on children and young people. The role of the media in the upbringing of children has never been as powerful. Mass media influences the clothes children and young people wear, how they behave, how they think and even the values that they attain. Messages are skilfully delivered to children and young people, who spend an average of three hours a day in front of the television. Corporate Australia, realising the high disposable income that adolescents have, spends billions of dollars on advertising aimed at this vulnerable, impressionable market. The insidious part about this is that at a time when a person's self-image is being shaped, they are bombarded with messages about the perfect body shape and exposed to role models they have little hope of copying.

The current crop of reality programs on television that use black humour and mindless cruelty, further pushes the concept of childhood underground. They also help to make the current group of teenagers surely the most cynical generation in history.

Combine these developments with high youth suicide rates, the incidence of alcohol and drug dependency, youth homelessness, increased youth crime rates and an increase in anti-social behaviour and it is natural to feel depressed about the future. But the resilience movement that has emerged from the United States points to optimism about the future. Its advocates have identified factors in human development that enable young people to bounce back and live fulfilling lives despite coming from difficult backgrounds or engaging in risk-taking behaviour as adolescents. Perhaps the prime lesson to learn from the resilience movement is that we need to work with young people's strengths rather than focus on their problems. While it is not about resilience, this book acknowledges the fact that young people can bounce back from less than ideal beginnings and celebrates the fact that if we work from strengths and provide kids with environments that offer care and support, positive expectations and opportunities for active participation, we have every right to be optimistic about the future.

There is nothing more powerful than an idea whose time has come. The time has come for parents and adults to re-enter the lives of children, not in controlling, critical ways but in nurturing, teaching, supportive, influential ways. The realisation is dawning that adults do make a difference in the lives of the next generation.

1

LEADING THE WAY

*Children are the messages we send to a future
that we shall never see.*

JONAS SALK

Raising a child is not a job for wimps. It takes courage, self-control, patience and often self-denial to raise children. It also takes character and strength. Perhaps that is why many adults consciously choose not have children these days.

Kids need to be surrounded by adults who are good leaders and good people, rather than effective managers. Most parents react with surprise when I remind them that they are leaders. As one mother put it at the end of a recent seminar, 'No one ever told me that I was leadership material.' Leadership is usually linked to politics, the sports field or the business world, rather than family life or teaching.

Make no mistake, parents and teachers are leaders for children. As significant adults in children's lives, you play an important part in shaping who they are and the type of people they become.

Many families are managed on the basis of a reaction to a crisis, or according to a whim or mood, rather than on the basis of a philosophy or a set of principles. The search for consistency that many parents battle with reflects a lack of understanding about what they want to achieve as parents and the qualities and characteristics they would like their children to develop.

LEARNING TO BE A PARENT

Current understandings indicate that parents construct their ideas about parenting from their own experiences of being parented, by interacting with their children, and from informal sources such as their peer groups.

Ghosts from the past

We generally bring a great deal of our own experience of being parented with us when we have children. It is eerie how at times we can hear our own parents speak through us. I not only hear my father's words recurring when my children are less than perfect, but also recognise his tone of voice and body language. And despite the fact that I swore that I would never lecture my children in the same manner as my father, I often catch myself giving a 'When I was your age'... type of lecture in the same manner as my dad. The ghosts from the past are very powerful.

Not only do we unwittingly raise children like our own parents did; our beliefs and values are often coloured by our experience of being parented. One young father I know was extremely concerned about his children's behaviour at mealtimes and overreacted when they misbehaved. His reaction at mealtime wasn't in line with his expectations of their behaviour at other times. After some reflection, he admitted that his behaviour was influenced by his unhappy experiences of childhood. So intent was he for mealtime to be enjoyable and harmonious that he overreacted when anything occurred to spoil his perfect vision.

One of the difficulties for step-parents is the lack of suitable role models in their own family of origin. If they were raised by their natural parents, the manner of the relationships they have with their step-children will be very different from their parents' relationships with them. It is little wonder that many step-parents find the experience of raising step-children both daunting and confusing.

Our peers

Our peer group has a strong influence on the way we raise children. We often use other children as yardsticks for measuring our children's development, academic performance and even their behaviour. We also tend to adopt the norms of the social groups that we mix with. If the people we admire and spend most time with are nurturing parents then we are more likely to treat our children the same way.

We often use our friends as reference points when we deal with our own children. I had the opportunity to witness some first-rate parenting at close quarters when we spent a two-week holiday with friends who had a testy fifteen-year-old. The young teenager tried to argue with his father over every little issue. Jackson, my friend, remained calm and ignored most of his son's surly behaviour, even when it was directed at him. I was impressed by his self-control, although I was a little dismayed at how he could sit back and let his son's criticisms of him wash over. Some time later I adopted a similar attitude when my own son began testing the waters and verbally challenging me, as teenage boys often do. I was able to recall my friend's controlled actions when dealing with his son and act in a similar way. It was good to have a reference point when new and challenging behaviours came along.

Learning on the run

There is no substitute for experience if we wish to gain an understanding of children and how best to meet their needs. Many first-borns rightfully point out that they are guinea-pigs leading their parents into new ground and paving the way for those siblings who follow. Eldest children give their parents their first taste of each stage of development. The moodiness that seems to come with adolescence often causes less concern if a parent has already experienced extreme emotional swings in an elder child. The lack of competence with kids that many fathers confess to is due more to lack of experience than any innate factors. Quite simply, because mothers usually spend more time involved in day-to-day parenting tasks than fathers, they often have a greater understanding of their children and their behaviours. Fathers need to become involved in as many aspects of child-rearing as possible so they can form bonds with their children and learn about the practicalities of raising them.

Formal sources

Increasingly, parents look for direction as well as information from professionals about how best to raise their children. Research indicates that parents are more likely to seek advice and assistance at times of significant change in kids' lives such as when they enter adolescence or at times of a marriage breakdown.

Parents need more. While many parents are looking for a roadmap or a set of instructions to assist with their parenting, what most need is a vision or a set of principles to assist them. Many parents tend to look back at their own parenting experiences for guidance or look around them at their peers or to experts for advice, but many forget to look ahead and formulate a vision about what values and characteristics they would like their children to develop.

START WITH THE END IN MIND

The most common question that parents ask during seminars relates to discipline: 'Should I smack my child?' This is a simple question with a myriad of implications. Smacking is a form of punishment or method of gaining compliance that parents often employ with children under five. It is quick, easy to apply and often achieves the desired result in terms of gaining compliance or a change in behaviour. So, in a behavioural sense, it is often (but not always) effective. However, that rationale still doesn't make it appropriate as a parenting practice.

The use of smacking indicates a great deal about a parent's beliefs about raising children. When people ask me about the appropriateness of smacking (as opposed to its effectiveness), I respond by asking people if they would inflict physical harm on their neighbour if he or she annoyed them or interfered with their privacy. Invariably, people respond in the negative, claiming that violence is an unacceptable way of resolving conflict or settling differences. Yet these same parents would inflict physical harm on their own children. This reflects deeper beliefs about the social equality of children and notions of the right of children to be treated with respect.

Parents often recall their own experiences of being disciplined with physical force, claiming that it didn't do them any harm. 'Spare the rod and spoil the child' may have been acceptable at one time but our society at the moment rejects this method of discipline.

Parents who take a leadership rather than a purely managerial viewpoint would ask what smacking teaches their children. What messages will the child internalise from being smacked and what does this say about the parent–child relationship? They would look past the immediate moment and take a longer term view of their actions.

Effective leaders in all walks of life take a long-term view of their activities. The difference between a leader and a manager is best illustrated in an analogy used by Steven Covey in his book *The Seven Habits of Highly Effective People*. He describes a group of people cutting a track through a jungle. The managers are busy urging the cutters on, devising health plans, working out schedules and generally concentrating on everyday procedures; they are very busy keeping the cutters on task and on track. The leader, however, is the person who climbs the tallest tree, surveys the area, and works out if they are heading in the right direction. The leader points the way for the others to follow.

This analogy is just as true for parenting as it is for work or other areas of life. Most of our time as parents is spent on management tasks – we remind kids to get up and get ready for school, devise rosters for chores, make lunches, and perform an endless range of management tasks. We also need to step back from routine managerial tasks on a regular basis to survey the broader scene and ask ourselves what type of children do we want? Are my children happy? Are we living the type of life that our children can emulate?

To begin with the end in mind means having a clear understanding of what you would like to achieve. In a parenting sense it means having a clear understanding of the type of adult you would like your child to be and the type of family you would like to have. What values, attitudes and character would you like your child to have? What would you like to put in his or her kitbag for life? Now this does not presuppose that the child doesn't have freedom to choose their thoughts, behaviours, attitudes and values as they grow.

A mark of adulthood is having values and beliefs that are separate from those of one's parents (although they maybe similar). But everything we do as parents – and what we neglect to do – influences the type of person our child becomes.

It is astonishing how the lessons of childhood often stay with a person or surface in adult life. Most people instinctively handle conflict as adults in much the same way as they did when they were kids. Okay, the noisy tantrums of a four-year-old may be replaced by a more sophisticated form of emotional blackmail known as sulking when we are adult. The purpose is still the same – to regain control. Perhaps as a child you learned to shout and overpower people to win an argument. Well, maybe as an adult you don't shout any more. Instead, you have learned the more subtle and effective skills of persuasion and argument to get your own way.

DEVELOPING A SHARED VISION FOR YOUR FAMILY

Good schools have a vision shared by all their staff and, hopefully, their students about what they wish to achieve. It is a statement about core values and philosophies that are reflected in everyday activities. One school, for example, promotes the three R's of respect for self, respect for the environment and respect for others. This philosophy influences all the staff interactions with children, its management practices, and even its curriculum design. It is evident in the student dress code, the physical layout of the school buildings and the way that staff members speak to each other and to students. It is a philosophy that is lived rather than a shallow, meaningless motto.

Parents too need some type of vision for their family and their children. Most parents I have met have positive aspirations for their children. Their hopes and dreams for their children lead many to work hard, to take a second job to provide the best possible opportunities for their children. The trouble is, few people have thought through their hopes and dreams – their vision about family life. And from my experience, even fewer have communicated any vision or set of beliefs with their partner. Subsequently, some parents are on totally different wavelengths when it comes to raising their children, which leads to inconsistency and confusion.

Developing a shared vision requires you to think about what is important to you about family life and your children. It involves discussion and communication with a partner and with children, if they are old enough to contribute. The vision or mission statement should be recorded so that it can be referred to and not forgotten. Importantly, it shouldn't be seen as a blueprint for living but more as an acknowledgment of the core values and beliefs that exist in your family.

FINDING AN APPROPRIATE MANAGEMENT STYLE

When I ask parents what they want their children to be five or ten years down the track I get various responses. Most answer that they want their children to be happy, independent and able to make their own mark on the world. I have a suspicion that a straw poll conducted anywhere in Australia would reveal a similar group of responses. The question is, What are you doing now to reach that end?

If parents want happy, responsible, self-disciplined children, they must keep this end in mind as they interact with them on a daily basis. One mother who admitted spoiling her seven-year-old son claimed that she wanted him to be an independent person capable of standing on his own two feet. This aim was not reflected in the way she raised her son. She indulged him by doing everything for him around the house. She got him up, packed his bag each morning and dutifully drove him to school. Nothing was expected of her son. This mother's management didn't reflect her aim. If she had said she wanted her son to be dependent and learn how to put others in his service then I would have agreed that she was going the right way about it.

The use of pocket money reflects a great deal about attitudes and family beliefs. Keith, a father of three school-aged children, linked his children's pocket money to chores. The more they did at home, the more money they received each week. Keith also had a number of concerns about his children. They competed heavily with each other in sport, at school and at home, and they constantly argued. More disturbingly, Keith claimed that his children were selfish, always looking out for themselves and showing little concern for the welfare of others, including their siblings. Keith's concerns were valid but he didn't realise that he was contributing both to his children's competitiveness and their 'what's in it for me' attitude by linking their help to pocket money. He wanted his children to learn that there was no such thing as a free lunch, but this lesson backfired. In the quest for money he set each child up against the other. This method taught them that cooperation comes at a price rather than through a wish to contribute. After reflecting on what was happening in his family, he changed his way of sharing the family wealth. He provided each child with an amount that reflected their age and needs and expected each to pull their weight around the house without being paid. He provided strong, thoughtful leadership that reflected what was happening at the time in his family and the type of values and attitudes he wanted to promote.

MANAGE YOURSELF

Good leaders focus on managing themselves rather than their children. When children misbehave or fail to cooperate, our first reaction is often to scold, remind or criticise. Our reaction will often depend on our mood at the time, the age of the child, which child (our reactions vary according to each child in the family) and the way we were disciplined as a child. We often react instinctively, particularly at the end of the day or when we are tired. Most parents I speak to admit that the battle for self-control is always present when interacting with kids. If we are to be effective leaders of children then we must first control ourselves rather than reacting to children; this is the challenge for parents and caregivers. If we are tired and control is an issue then withdrawal is usually the best technique to use. This may mean going for a walk or phoning a friend to give you a break if the children are too young to be unsupervised. Getting away is easier when children are older and supervision is less of an issue.

LEAD BY EXAMPLE – THE POWER OF MODELLING

Effective leaders in all walks of life know that the behaviour they model has the greatest impact on those around them. Ninety to ninety-five per cent of all human learning occurs through modelling; only five to ten per cent occurs from explicit or verbal directions of the 'do this, don't do that' variety. That is an astounding statistic. Modelled learning is largely unconscious, picked up from non-verbal behaviour and is strongly influenced by the quality of the relationship that exists between the learner and the model. E. Timothy Burns in *From Risk to Resilience* reminds us of our responsibility to children when he says, 'So if ninety-nine percent of our learning is modelled we need to focus on ourselves as models: the kind of life we are living and the example we set.'

Twentieth century poet Edgar Guest expressed the significance of modelling in his poem 'The Living Sermon':

> *I'd rather see a sermon, than to hear one any day.*
> *I'd rather one should walk with me than to merely show the*
> > *way*
> *I can soon learn how to do it, if you'd let me see it done.*
> *I can watch your hands in action but your tongue too fast*
> > *may run.*
> *All the lectures you deliver may be very wise and true,*
> *But I'd rather get my lesson by observing what you do.*
> *Though I might not understand you and the fine advice you*
> > *give.*
> *There's no misunderstanding how you act and how you live.*

The impact of modelling by parents and other significant adults on children is profound. In a way, we are only beginning to discover the power of positive and negative role modelling. It is all-pervasive, affecting our thoughts, behaviour, attitudes and values. An anti-alcohol advertisement on Australian television in the early 1990s was a terrific demonstration of the effects of parental modelling. The advertisement showed two preschool-aged children playing mothers and fathers in their cubbyhouse. It was a scene that is familiar to many, but one that wouldn't put a smile on the face of too many feminists. The young girl was busily preparing the evening meal while a young boy sat at the kitchen table drinking a bottle of beer. When the girl asked the boy to go to the shop to buy some milk he replied, 'Yeah, no worries. Just wait until I knock off another one.' Fathers around Australia would have cringed at that advertisement, but the tag at the end was most poignant: 'Every move you make someone is watching.'

CHILDREN ARE ACUTE OBSERVERS

It is amazing the little things that kids notice. My two daughters revealed one day their secret way of working out whether their mother or I make their school lunches. They boasted a perfect track record – we could make identical lunches with similar snacks and they knew who prepared them. We even wrapped the sandwiches in an identical manner and they still knew.

The secret, they revealed, was in the way we cut the sandwiches: my wife Sue cut them diagonally while I cut in parallel lines. Always, no deviation. Until now, that is.

We know that children are acute observers of what happens around them but we just don't quite know what they are taking in or what they are focusing on. What is quite a mundane behaviour for adults may be of extreme importance for kids. We are models for kids but which of our behaviours, beliefs and values they adopt and what they ignore or discard is hard to fathom. Whether we like it or not our attitudes, our values, our language and our behaviour are on show for children.

LEADERS ARE NEVER OFF DUTY

Because we don't quite know what kids are taking in, parents and other significant adults are never off duty. I conduct leadership seminars for students and they always feel distinctly uneasy when I discuss this concept with them. They realise that if they want to be taken seriously as school and house captains they must act like leaders as soon as they leave home in the morning. They never know when they are being observed so they need to model appropriate behaviours at all times.

The expectation for parents is not necessarily to be the perfect mother or father who never loses control and is always cool in a crisis. It means that parents must strive to be the best possible person that they can be. That is a big ask for many parents, but, as I said at the start of this chapter, raising kids is not for wimps or the faint-hearted. Parenting is the most adult activity you will ever do. When we mess up or blow our tops at our children then an apology is the best response. It is important to remember that we are presenting a particular view to children. Consider the following: Are you the type of person that you want your kids to copy? Is the way you treat them and others the way that you want them to treat each other on a regular basis?

DON'T CRIPPLE THEM WITH YOUR ATTITUDES

It is amazing how even very young children pick up our attitudes. One mother told me how her daughter had picked up on the pessimistic attitude that she and her husband constantly displayed. Both parents saw setbacks as obstacles or problems rather than opportunities, which was reflected in their language when things went wrong. Their four-year-old daughter also complained when things went wrong, echoing the words her parents used as well as their body language and tone of voice.

Another three-year-old I know who is blessed with an optimistic mother has picked up her mother's optimistic view of the world. When she broke a valuable plate when visiting her grandparents she claimed, 'Ah, it's broke. It doesn't matter. Pa will fix it.' Okay, this was optimistic to the point of being unrealistic, however it reflected a positive view that she had picked up from her parents.

CONGRUENCY – DO AS I DO

Your own life needs to be congruent with what you expect from your children. If children are to develop a respect for others and a set of acceptable values then parents and teachers must live those values themselves, not just give them lip service.

This is tough. I once lied about the age of one of my children when we went to see a film. I put the age of my child down a year to save paying the adult admission charge. I rationalised it by saying that twelve was too young to have to pay an adult price so I kept my conscience clean. A couple of weeks later my son asked me to write a note to his teacher asking for an extension to a homework assignment. He wanted me to write that he had been too ill to do his homework. When I pointed out that he was asking me to lie for him he reminded me that I had been less than honest at the movies a couple of weeks earlier. He had me cold. We need to 'walk our talk' with children.

Our behaviour rather than our words is important in other areas too. For instance, if parents want their children to watch less television and read more then they will have more success if they set the example. The British have put positive role modelling to good effect in their efforts to encourage school-aged boys to read more. Researchers found that boys viewed reading as a 'female activity' as their mothers were more likely to read at home than fathers were. The latter chose either more active (outdoor) pastimes or more sedentary (television-viewing) pursuits. To change the prevailing attitude that it was not cool or masculine for boys to read, fathers across the land have been encouraged to switch off the television and read more for their own pleasure as well as to their sons.

Similarly, it is pointless reminding adolescents to drink alcohol sensibly if we drink to excess ourselves or even to admonish them to keep a tidy bedroom if we keep ours like a pig sty. Kids of all ages are quick to pick up on the double standards of adults and are enduringly influenced by our behaviour.

PERSONAL QUALITIES COUNT

Norman Schwarzkopf, the leader of the US troops in the Gulf War of the early 1990s, was asked what he looked for in a good leader. He replied with one word: character. Schwarzkopf believed a leader needed strong personal qualities such as self-discipline, reliability and loyalty. While raising kids is not akin to leading people into a war zone, although doubtless some parents would disagree, children benefit from being around people who are of good character and who possess an array of strong personal qualities. Too often we focus on the strategies we use when managing children rather than the qualities and integrity of the person with whom children interact.

A number of years ago my wife and I looked around for a carer to mind our three young children. Choosing someone to look after your children is no easy task. There were many aspects to consider, including the proximity of the carer to the children's school and our home, the activities she provided, and the number and age of her own children. However, these considerations, although relevant, were far less important than the character and personal qualities of the carer. The person we eventually chose had had little experience of looking after other people's children but had plenty of enthusiasm and human warmth. It was an intuitive decision. The moment I entered her home I felt welcome and safe. Her personal skills were excellent as she had the knack of making me feel at ease. Both my wife and I thought she was a person of excellent character and terrific personal qualities who would have not only our children's best interests at heart but something lasting to contribute. Our hunch was right. She was a wonderful carer whom the children adored because she had a genuine interest in their well-being and some wonderful personal qualities as well.

GOOD COMMUNICATION IS THE KEY

Mastery of communication is what makes a great parent or a
great artist or a great politician or a great teacher.
ANTHONY ROBBINS

The people who influence and shape our lives are invariably master communicators. They share their ideas, their visions or their stories in ways that make us listen and even follow. Most problems in families, whether between parents and children or between siblings, are linked to communication difficulties. If parents are to improve one skill area of their lives it is the vital area of communication skills. How parents speak to and how they listen to their children and each other is a key to leading successful families.

It has long fascinated me how some people can gain cooperation from very difficult children whereas others gain little cooperation, cause an argument or merely ignite children's anger. I'm sure you have encountered teachers and parents who seem to have the knack of getting through to kids while others just put them offside. Gaining cooperation is more than just luck. It reflects good communication.

A couple I know with two children are at the opposite ends of the communication spectrum. The relationship they each have with their two school-aged children reflects this. Jenny is a wonderful communicator who considers her children's needs before she opens her mouth. She talks softly and politely to her children and gains cooperation by asking for help rather than barking out orders. Her husband, Roger, has a difficult time gaining cooperation from his children. He expects everything to be done yesterday and his children are generally unwilling helpers. They usually procrastinate when given a task or argue about unfairness or some other issue. Roger expressed his frustration to me: 'When Jenny asks the children to stack the dishwasher, hang their towels up or to do some job they will both do it immediately. But they won't do anything for me without a fight. Where am I going wrong?'

The difference was in the communication methods that each parent used. I have closely observed the way Jenny interacts with her children, particularly when she wants some help. She usually smiles, makes eye contact, lowers her voice and asks rather than demands compliance. She will even touch her children gently on the arm or the shoulder if she is close enough. Her tone of voice and body language are friendly yet convey an expectation of cooperation. Roger's tone of voice, body language and even his choice of words when speaking to his children are more likely to be harsh and aggressive. Roger got quite a shock when I told him that there is no way I would help him out if he spoke to me like he spoke to his children. The way he spoke might have reflected a deeper held belief that children should do as they are told regardless of how they are approached. He clearly expected obedience on demand, which showed through his language. His parents might have spoken to him this way when he was young. If Roger wanted a little more cooperation, he needed to start with better communication. Jenny used the communication skills required of a leader while Roger used outmoded managerial-type language that didn't have the desired effect.

LEADERS VALUE RELATIONSHIPS

Stephen Covey has good advice for parents who struggle to balance their time between family, work and other commitments. Covey believes that if relationships are to be successful, those involved must build up a strong emotional bank account through shared, positive experiences. Parents build up goodwill with their children through listening, encouraging, talking and doing those nurturing activities that are generally considered part of the job. According to Covey, the more positive experiences parents share with their children, the stronger their relationships are likely to be. When parents show discourtesy or disrespect, ignore kids or are simply too busy getting on with their lives to spend time with them the emotional bank account becomes overdrawn. Covey's emotional bank account concept is forgiving for parents because we can put back what we take out, but it takes effort and time to make the necessary deposits. (See figure 1.)

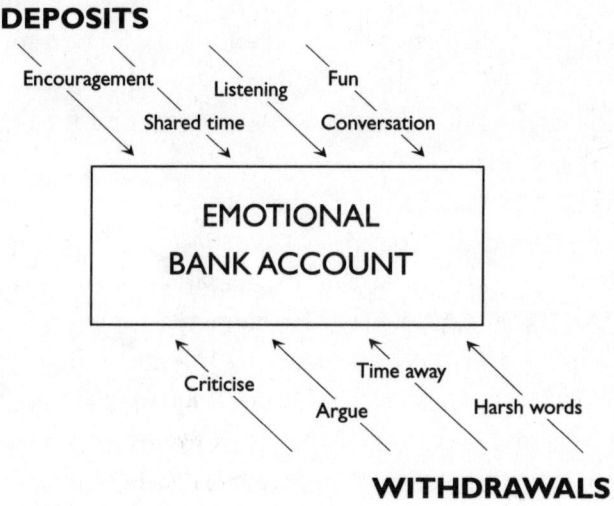

Figure 1: The emotional bank account

PARENTS AND TEACHERS NEED ROLE MODELS TOO

It is relatively easy for Roger to learn better ways of communicating with his children because he has an excellent role model living under the same roof. He only has to sit back and observe how his wife interacts with their children and adapt those same techniques to suit his personal style. If his desire to change is sincere and strong enough he can learn better ways of communicating.

The same holds true for any parent or teacher. If you are having difficulty getting your child to listen to you, having problems gaining compliance or just want to have a conversation that elicits more than a grunt then observe a good communicator first hand and copy them. It sounds ridiculously simple but the skills of communication can be learned. Find a good communicator; observe them interacting with their children. Listen to their choice of words and their tone of voice. Watch the body language they use, their use of touch, their facial expressions. Copy their behaviour in your everyday interactions with your children.

The hard part for many people is being exposed to a good communicator. If you are surrounded by people who constantly criticise their children and each other and use the language of compliance rather than cooperation then you lack good role models. Look for models of excellence and learn from them. Other parents, teachers and even children can be good role models for the way you interact with children.

As a first year primary teacher many years ago I really struggled to make the grade. My experience of primary-age children was limited and teacher training was heavy on lecture content and light on providing hands-on experience. My own experiences as a student in primary school were irrelevant as teaching methodology had shifted dramatically from a didactic to a more experiential model in that time. As a young teacher I looked around my new school for guidance and I latched onto an experienced male teacher in a similar grade level to mine. As a role model he was inadequate, as he was authoritarian and quite cruel in his treatment of children. It was testimony to the power of modelling that despite my reservations about his communication style I soon became a carbon copy of my role model. Fortunately, there was a young male teacher in the school whom I admired. He was loved by the children and respected by the staff. He was a quiet communicator who didn't appear to become ruffled or stressed under the intense pressure of noisy classroom life. I didn't realise how much I had noticed this quiet communicator until the end of the year holidays when I backpacked around South East Asia. To pass the time travelling on buses and trains I would visualise how I would teach my class the following school year. I found myself copying in my mind the communication style of the colleague whom I admired. I imagined myself mimicking his mannerisms, his phrases and even the tone of voice that he used. When I returned to classroom work I found that I had adopted a whole new set of skills. Colleagues remarked that I had returned from my trip a new person. They were wrong. I wasn't a new person, I just used new skills gained by recalling the actions of a much-admired role model. As I gained in competence in my interactions with children I slowly adopted my own unique way of communicating based on what I learned through my observations.

2

CREATING HEALTHY ENVIRONMENTS FOR KIDS

Sow a thought and you reap an act;
Sow an act and you reap a habit;
Sow a habit and you reap a character;
Sow a character and you reap a destiny.

RALPH WALDO EMERSON

CHARACTERISTICS OF HEALTHY FAMILIES

In the consideration of positive family environments for kids, debate often revolves around family type or shape. Experts often argue the merits of dual-parent families over sole-parent families, compare intact families to stepfamilies or weigh up the comparative merits of having one or both parents in the paid work force. This narrow type of focus is unhelpful for children and parents. It is more useful to focus on characteristics that may exist in a family regardless of its type, shape or its socioeconomic status.

THE RESILIENCE MOVEMENT

The 'resilience movement' is a term for the ideas and concepts espoused by Bonnie Benard, E. Timothy Burns, Glenn Richardson and others from the youth work, prevention and education field in the USA.

This movement has identified family characteristics that underpin the development of resilient individuals and that are powerful predictors of positive outcomes for kids. While this may be a minimalist approach to raising children, it is a good baseline to establish in attempting to develop environments that will enable kids to become positive, productive individuals capable of dealing with life's difficulties and dilemmas. These characteristics fall into three categories:

- caring and support
- positive expectations
- opportunities for participation.

Caring and support

Children and young people need a stable relationship with at least one parent in their family who can offer love and verbal and physical affection if they are to develop inner strengths and competencies. Studies of children who have lived in the most stressful circumstances such as with an alcoholic or abusing parent show the importance of one healthy adult in their lives. When there is at least one adult who takes an interest in and invests time in a child then the child's chances of living a fulfilled life increase dramatically.

Positive expectations

The expectations that parents have for their children become a self-fulfilling prophecy. Expect too little of them and they generally won't disappoint us. If we verbally criticise children and point out their ineptitude, worthlessness or incompetence, we set kids up for failure.

Positive expectations for children's performance set in motion an often astonishing train of events where children will often defy their apparent abilities and produce results that meet the positive expectations. The key to positive expectations according to researchers such as Roger Mills and Bonnie Benard is to establish them when children are very young.

Researchers warn that parents who hold up excessive or rigid expectations for kids to aspire to are in danger of inviting them to give up and turn to misbehaviour as a way of belonging to their family. The key word is 'positive' rather than 'high' expectations.

Opportunities for participation

In a healthy family, children are able to contribute to the well-being of the family and participate in ways that add meaning to their own lives. Participation in chores, helping to care for siblings and having input into decisions that affect the family are character building for children. Participation also reinforces the notion that children are worthwhile and valuable and promotes the value of cooperation.

THE CHARACTERISTICS OF RESILIENT INDIVIDUALS

The three protective factors discussed above promote four characteristics or traits that are commonly found in resilient individuals – people who are able to bounce back from adversity. These are:

- social competence: relationship and communication skills
- problem-solving skills: including the ability to plan, help others, find and use resources and think critically
- autonomy: the ability to act independently and exert control over a person's environment
- a sense of purpose: goals, direction motivation and a sense of future.

ESTABLISHING ENVIRONMENTS TO PROMOTE RESILIENCE IN CHILDREN

The environment children grow up in impacts on their growth and development. Educators the world over have in the last few decades recognised that a child's home environment has a significant influence on their learning potential. For instance, children who grow up in a language-rich environment where their parents talk with them, read with them and provide them with opportunities to practise their language skills will have a far greater chance of success in literacy when they begin school.

Effective teachers are not merely good instructors; they establish stimulating environments that facilitate children's learning. A multitude of factors make up an effective learning environment, including the quality and quantity of the materials available, the quality of the instructors, the methods they use and the atmosphere that pervades the room. By far the most influential factor in a good learning environment is the quality of the teacher who created it. When people discuss their school days, few talk about the equipment that existed in the school or whether the books were modern or the sport-shed was well stocked. Memories and stories always revolve around people, particularly the teachers who left either a positive or a negative impression on them: 'That old Mr Smith. He was a cow. I remember one time he...' or 'Miss Jones was terrific. She was a real softie. You could always go to her if you had a problem.' Teachers are by far the most significant part of a good learning environment at school.

The environment that parents create at home can either promote a child's healthy development or stunt their emotional and social growth and hinder their potential. It is not the material things, the toys and the computers that contribute to a healthy home environment; rather, it is the atmosphere that parents help to create that has a lasting impact. Both mothers and fathers influence the mood and the atmosphere in their homes by the way they interact with each other and their children.

What type of atmosphere do you create in your home? Is the pervading atmosphere one of encouragement or one of criticism? Is it warm and friendly or cold and unforgiving? Do you greet your children with a smile or are they more than likely to see a growl or snarl on your face? Do you expect too little or too much of your child? Is laughter a regular part of your interactions with kids or are they more than likely to see you frown? Do you whinge about events that happen to you or do you take a positive attitude when life is less than ideal?

Your behaviour influences the atmosphere that children experience. Tom, an eloquent eighteen-year-old, told me how his father's mood influenced the atmosphere in his family.

'If he was happy, which largely depended on his day at work, then home life was fine. He would be all smiles, full of chat and very playful. But all too frequently he would come home from work in a bad mood. And his mood hung over the family like a heavy cloud.

When he got into one of his moods anything was likely to happen, so no one dared to make a noise or disturb him for fear of being criticised or abused. Living with my old man was like living with a box of explosives and never knowing if the wick was alight or not.'

No-one is immune from disappointments and difficulties. Every day we experience all sorts of upsets, both minor and potentially debilitating. I am not suggesting that we keep problems to ourselves and not share them with our family, but we need to deal with them in positive ways rather than let them fester and negatively influence the atmosphere that exists at home. Parents who are leaders don't necessarily shield children from life's adversities, but they don't allow their mood or their experiences to impact negatively on their children. As difficult as this may be, it is the price of parenthood.

Most parents sell themselves short and underestimate the influence they have on children. During my seminars, many parents tell me that their children take more notice of their peers than they do of them or they use characters on television programs as reference points. This can be particularly disconcerting for those parents raising adolescents. Certainly as children reach adolescence our direct influence dwindles as they begin to forge their own ideas and go their own way. After all, the task for an adolescent is to stand on her or his own two feet as an individual. But parents as significant people in a child's environment leave a lasting impression. Interestingly, many young adults adopt similar values and attitudes to their parents after spending much of their adolescence trying to exert their individuality by being as different as possible from their parents.

Effective leaders create a family environment where children build a positive sense of self, a sense of teamwork and a sense of self-discipline.

CHALLENGE 1: BUILDING A POSITIVE SENSE OF SELF

Parents need to establish an atmosphere at home where children feel valued, safe and respected.

One day, a woman approached me at the end of a seminar and told me about her childhood. As a child she was impeccably clean, neat and tidy. She was very quiet and spent most of her spare time reading. She had no doubt that she was the cleanest kid that ever lived. Her bedroom was spotless, her schoolbooks didn't have a mark of scribble or graffiti and her clothes were always freshly ironed. She lived, however, in an atmosphere devoid of warmth and full of criticism. Nothing she did was ever good enough for either of her parents. They only expressed approval when she was eating ('she has a wonderful appetite') or reading ('she's always got her nose stuck in a book'). As a result, she grew up with a weight problem, an extensive vocabulary and few social skills. With help and a great deal of effort she turned her life around as she realised she had the power to choose how she thought and behaved. As a mother to her daughters she was the opposite to her own parents. She created a warm, loving atmosphere at home built on approval and encouragement. As a result, her daughters are, according to her, 'charming, very popular, confident... everything I would like to be, but never will be'.

The family atmosphere that this woman grew up in was toxic rather than positive. Criticism rather than approval, and control rather than free will, were the mainstays of the family environment which influenced the way she saw herself both as a child and as an adult.

Helping kids feel safe

Kids of all ages are more likely to develop their full potential if they live in an environment that is physically and psychologically safe. A child's right to adequate physical care and to live in a family environment free from violence and physical abuse has been enshrined by legislation in many parts of the world. They are seen as basic human rights. Parents can help children feel safe by taking adequate care and supervision procedures and by refraining from physical punishment. They need to do more.

Kids should feel psychologically safe as well. They need to grow up in an atmosphere free from the threat of abuse or punishment and free from criticism or embarrassment when they make mistakes or misbehave.

The courage to be imperfect

Parents can develop an atmosphere at home where mistakes of all types are okay and not a mark of failure. Rudolf Dreikurs, author of *Children: The Challenge* and an influential figure in family and child psychology in the 1950s and 1960s, urged adults to develop in children the courage to be imperfect. Further, he claimed that the adulation of and indeed the quest for perfection that is prevalent in western society inhibits the individual's potential. Although he stated these views over thirty years ago, a quick glance through any magazine will demonstrate that they are just as relevant today.

He reasoned that children will only extend themselves and reach their full potential if they take risks as learners and try different activities or new ways of doing things. When children take risks then mistakes are inevitable. As any sports person knows, mistakes are part of the learning process. In a world where the perfect body, the perfect performance and the perfect job are celebrated, it can take a great deal of courage to go out on a limb and make a few blunders. I am not suggesting that we lower our standards of kids' performance or that quality is not important. Perfection has its place; the makers of condoms and parachutes had better get it right. But an attitude that is intolerant of mistakes and blunders and insists that only the best will do at all times hinders rather than helps kids. Due to their own upbringing and their educational experiences, many adults have developed an aversion to making errors. In fact, for many of us our entire existence consists of avoiding errors, slip-ups or unintended blunders.

The folly of the child improvement cult

Some parents will do anything to avoid their child being average or ordinary. The current child development culture that exists in many parts of Australia has an aversion to average achievement. A huge industry now exists that pays homage to parents' ambitions to have not just a well-rounded child but an achieving child. Kids from as young as three can have their entire week filled with self-improvement activities from ballet through to computer lessons. It is common for many school-aged children to have a full schedule of after-school and weekend activities that make sure that they have few idle moments.

Kids are tested and tagged as potential achievers from as young as four and attend gifted children's enrichment programs to make sure their potential is not wasted. The pressures of achievement which are placed on them by adults pervade childhood to such an extent that children can now take organised relaxation classes which teach them how to handle stress.

Failure is not an option for many children these days. If a child's marks are down in a particular area at school there is intense pressure to improve or make up those marks. Scant regard is given to kids' interests and to the fact that they may not be strong in certain areas. It can be hard to realise that a child may not be the scholarly type or may be better in some areas than others, or that children develop at different rates. Academic problems don't always need to be fixed: sometimes improvement simply comes with age and maturation. But in the era of the quick fix and corporatised child-raising, low achievers can be assessed and receive catch-up classes or extra tuition to bring them up to scratch. Nothing is left to chance.

The present panic over literacy levels is an example of the current dilemma that many parents find themselves facing. Some parents have spent thousands of dollars to improve their children's literacy even when no problem exists. Many children attend preschool drama and language classes for the best possible start or they go to kindergartens that boast high academic programs over those that promote more traditional social skills. When problems appear their parents will seek out paediatricians and diagnosis of attention deficit hyperactivity disorder (ADHD), they will organise home-tutor programs and even hire specially trained nannies to help improve literacy skills. All this when informed, rational educational opinion says that the most significant way a parent can promote reading is to read with a child for as little as fifteen minutes a day.

After-school programs and activities do offer much for children but there desperately needs to be some balance restored. Children of all ages need to be able to play, read and enjoy the company of themselves, their siblings and their parents free from the pressures of constantly having to perform and achieve.

CHALLENGE 2: BUILDING A SENSE OF TEAMWORK

Real belonging for children comes from contribution rather than a belief that they are the centre of their family.

Creating the conditions where families develop a sense of teamwork is a challenge for most parents. If your ideal notion of a family is one where children never argue, always look out for one another and never entertain a jealous thought when a sibling experiences success, you will probably be sorely disappointed. Families are like a can full of worms. In the process of finding their own place to feed they will crawl over and bump into each other. Sometimes they will end up in a tangled mess, but they all survive and grow fat. Like those worms, children will often collide head on in an effort to have their needs met and find their place in the family.

Alfred Adler, the father of individual psychology, believed that we are primarily social beings and as such our behaviour is motivated by our need to belong to the significant groups in our lives. We will belong to a group in two ways: by making a positive contribution to its ongoing well-being or through destructive ways if we feel inadequate or unable to contribute or that our contributions are devalued.

Have you ever been on a committee where your contribution was ignored or even ridiculed? If you have, the chances are you soon began to act in ways that didn't enhance the committee's agenda. You might have inadvertently acted in quite destructive ways. Perhaps you began to miss meetings or turned up late and left early. Maybe you tried to exert some authority by issuing a direct challenge to the chairperson or leader of the group, or perhaps you disagreed with the group's activities in private or bad-mouthed fellow committee members. This type of behaviour usually occurs when we don't feel we can make a positive contribution to a group.

Similarly, in a family setting children will belong through two ways: either through the ability to contribute and impact positively on family-life or through misbehaviour. Make no mistake, the 'black sheep', the pest or the behaviour-problem child has just as significant a place in their family as those who contribute positively. Everyone certainly knows that they are around.

It may come as a rude shock to some children, but effective families don't revolve around the needs of any one person. Common purpose rather than individual needs forms the axle around which families revolve. Unfortunately, many families are highjacked to the point that most of their activities revolve around the interests of one or two children.

Families need effective leadership if they are to develop a sense of teamwork based around a common purpose or common good. Sometimes an event such as a death in the family or a protracted illness to a parent or child will galvanise everyone to develop a feeling of common purpose. There are numerous examples of children pulling together like a finely tuned team to make sure family life runs smoothly when a parent has a long-term illness. Petty squabbles recede, reluctant helpers pull their weight and life goes on often more smoothly than ever.

Parents can develop a sense of teamwork by promoting the principle of contribution and the twin values of cooperation and mutual respect at every opportunity.

The basic principle of family leadership is that children belong to their families through contribution. This is a fine principle but how do we put it into practice or make our management fit the principle? Children contribute to the well-being of their families in the following ways:

- by having input into decision-making (for example, through family meetings)
- by providing assistance that benefits others
- by looking after their own well-being.

Formal meetings

A regular family meeting is an effective way of unifying a family and developing a shared approach to its organisation. Through regular meetings, the responsibility of running family life is shared among its members. This doesn't mean that parents shirk their responsibility; rather, it provides children with the opportunity on a regular basis to have some input into decision-making.

Family meetings sound like hard work

The term meeting has negative connotations associated with the workplace and the boardroom. Anecdotal evidence suggests that few Australian families conduct family meetings on a regular basis. In a way, this is due more to a busy lifestyle that makes timetabling such events difficult and an aversion to formality than to a rejection of democratic notions of parenting. Anecdotal evidence suggests that family meetings are highly successful in terms of promoting family harmony, reducing sibling fighting and promoting a cooperative spirit in children. Meetings are worth the effort.

Family meetings or forums take many forms but the most successful are those held regularly rather than on a needs basis – that is, once a week or once a fortnight. They follow an agenda containing a few items, have set time limits and conclude with an enjoyable activity such as a game or story. They provide opportunities for genuine discussion rather than just acting as a vehicle for parents to get a point across or gain compliance from children.

It is easier to begin conducting family meetings when children are primary school-aged. Those parents who begin with toddlers or preschool-aged children often give up in frustration, as children don't possess the skills to attend and contribute. When starting out, parents need to take a strong lead, be patient, set some simple rules and always begin with encouragement. It is important not to allow them to slip into gripe sessions where everyone criticises everyone else. Parents need to promote a positive outlook when problems are presented and provide children with the chance to talk about enjoyable activities such as where to go for an outing.

Meetings are not always successful. Some meetings in my family have been disasters where children have taken off to their rooms because the discussion has become personal. That is the way of life. But as an ongoing process that gives children a chance to air their grievances in a legitimate forum and have some impact on what happens in a family, regular meetings are effective.

While many parents provide children with input into family decision-making through discussions or through the TTOTR (talk together on the run) method, this is not as effective at promoting a real sense of purpose as family meetings. The TWS (talk while seated) approach is far more effective.

Resurrect the kitchen table

Modern household design has a lot to answer for in terms of its negative effects on family communication. The emergence of the breakfast bench where everyone sits in a line eating their meals and the decline in the popularity of the kitchen table is one practical factor that has contributed to a breakdown in communication.

One of the side-effects of our often frantic lives is that we are so busy these days attending to a multitude of activities that we don't often sit down and talk with each other. We are often just too busy. Conversations occur on the run or in the car while children are transported from one sports event or after-school activity to another.

I am not sure if architects of the past had family communication in mind when they designed their homes but the notion of making the kitchen the centre promoted effective communication. In many homes of past generations the epicentre of the kitchen would be a large table, generally strewn with food, books and notices. Here a great deal of family life would be conducted, with children sitting down to eat, chat, do homework or just drop in. Invariably, family life buzzed around the kitchen table. It was vibrant, it was lively and it generally occurred while at least one member was sitting on a chair, which meant they were relaxed and more likely to attend to others – and there was no television to distract them.

Promoting cooperation

The level of harmony in a family is often measured by the amount of conflict that occurs between siblings or parents and children. One popular view is that if there are few fights and arguments then the family is in great shape. If we used sibling fighting as a barometer then the majority of Australian families would be labelled as dysfunctional. My own research indicates that the amount and intensity of children's squabbles and disagreements disturbs approximately eighty per cent of parents.

I am commonly asked for ideas about managing sibling fighting, which focuses on the management perspective: 'What should I do when my child comes to me and complains that his brother or sister is picking on him?' 'How should I react when my children argue?' As managers, many parents look for ways of reducing sibling fighting.

It is better to measure family harmony by the amount of help and assistance children provide for each other and the amount of time that they spend either passively or actively enjoying each other's company. Parents as leaders need to be proactive in providing children with opportunities to help each other. Often children will compete with each other or boast about their performance in an effort to prove their worth at the expense of a sibling.

JONATHON AND STEVE

Nine-year-old Jonathon was a capable reader while Steve, his younger brother, struggled. Jonathon spent a great deal of his energy boasting about his skills as a reader while criticising his brother's efforts. The boys' mother was concerned at the spiralling effect the put-downs were having on Steve's willingness to read. Rather than try to manage Jonathon's put-down behaviour, she took a proactive approach. She acknowledged Jonathon's abilities as a reader and asked for his continued assistance to help his brother to improve his reading. Jonathon, with some initial training, became Steve's reading coach, hearing him read every night. Jonathon learned how to encourage his little brother's efforts and took pride in his young brother's eventual improvement. Jonathon didn't have to compete with his brother to show his worth. This showed proactive leadership by the boys' mother.

How to foster a sense of cooperation
Model cooperative behaviour

Parents need to model cooperation through their everyday interactions sending the message through their behaviour that kids help each other out in their family.

Don't compare siblings

One way to ensure that siblings compete rather than cooperate is to compare one sibling with another. When you hold up the behaviour of one child to be copied by another you are effectively driving a wedge between them. Comments such as 'Why can't you keep your room tidy like your sister?' or 'If you would only spend some time shooting goals you would improve like your brother' divide siblings and make cooperation difficult.

Recognise cooperative behaviour

Effective leaders don't take other people's efforts for granted. Everyone wants recognition for the things they do. If we help out then it is great to receive a word or two of appreciation. A friend who is an executive in a corporate environment gives his colleagues an animal stamp to show his appreciation for their efforts. He claims they love it because it is immediate and has a personal touch.

Effective family leaders are adept at recognising their children's cooperative behaviours. You can show your appreciation verbally, non-verbally with a smile, by giving, a 'thumbs up' or a hug or, even better, using a combination of verbal and non-verbal behaviour which encourages the cooperative behaviour to continue. We all know this but we so often forget to recognise the good stuff that children (and adults) do.

Chores, chores, chores

In the past when families were large and households had few labour-saving devices, children's help was essential. A mother's day was usually spent performing a range of household duties and children were expected to help out. In this era of small families and large machines many kids don't have the same opportunity to pitch in and help – or at least the necessity isn't quite as great – so many children don't have the opportunity to belong to their families by making a realistic contribution to its well-being. Interestingly, many parents today try a variety of methods to coerce children into helping out. Strategies such as linking allowances to chores or offering rewards and stickers to entice children are common in many homes. Such methods are often successful in terms of eliciting help, but they also teach children to think about what is in it for them rather than how they can make a contribution and how they can help. It is the principle of contribution and the value of cooperation that are significant rather than the simple completion of tasks.

So how do you get children to help out? The most significant aspect is an expectation that chores will be done. As one mother in a seminar replied when we were discussing methods for ensuring that kids help out, 'My kids just do their jobs because that is what you do in our family. If they don't do them no-one else will. We are not playing games here. I'm busy, they're busy I know, but I need their help. It's as simple as that.' Later this mother explained how she developed a helping habit in her children from an early age. She broke large jobs into small tasks to encourage them to contribute. Her children at around three years of age used to make their beds by smoothing the doona and arranging the teddies. They progressed from there. This mother also joined her children in making beds, tidying up and generally helping out, which was time-consuming but worth the effort in the long run.

Delegate to older children

Children become bored with chores and the novelty of helping wears off as they progress through primary school and move into adolescence. There is little doubt that developing helping habits in children at a young age supported by an expectation of compliance can have a lasting effect, but sometimes kids need more. One way leaders can use chores to promote a sense of responsibility and rekindle interest is through real delegation. This means giving total responsibility for an area such as putting out the garbage or keeping a backyard tidy. Try doing this without reminding or nagging them – that is the test of real delegation.

Looking after themselves

Never regularly do for a child what a child can do for him
or herself.

MAURICE BALSON

Children are very capable if we only provide them with plenty of opportunities to care for themselves. Often in our rush to get things done we inadvertently take on children's responsibilities as our own. We pack their school lunches, get them up in the morning and even take them to school when they are capable of doing these activities themselves.

A child's level of contribution depends on such factors as their age and stage of development and other issues such as level of schooling and outside interests that impacts on their ability to help.

3

DISCIPLINE WITHOUT TEARS, FEAR OR PUT-DOWNS

Children have never been very good at listening to their elders, but they have never failed to imitate them.

JAMES BALDWIN

Discipline is an extremely evocative but misunderstood term. Say the word aloud and you will probably conjure up images of punishment, criticism, embarrassment and other negative experiences. It is generally equated with physical punishment such as smacking, particularly by adults who were punished in such a way themselves as children. It is frequently connected with children's compliance to adult wishes or, alternatively, adult control over a child.

Discipline has lost much of its original meaning. It is a legitimate task of parenting and child-raising that helps children learn socially-acceptable forms of behaviour. Effective discipline has teaching as a focus rather than punishment. In a sense the discipline process helps children fit into their many social groups by helping them to be likeable and to be accepted by others.

Whenever the topic of discipline arises, whether in conversation, at a seminar or during a press interview, it invariably leads to the contentious issue of smacking. People usually want to know my opinion of smacking. I think that many parents want reassurance that it is okay to smack their children sometimes. Many people tell me that they don't really like to smack but they will do so as a last resort. The last resort concept is interesting as it tells children just how far a parent is willing to go. Often people cite the fact that they were disciplined in such a way when they were young and presumably it did them no harm.

The discipline that parents and carers use with children should always reflect the social mores of the era. My own parents didn't use physical punishment of any kind, however some of the teachers in my primary school used corporal punishment in fairly liberal doses. Physical punishment was an acceptable form of discipline in the 1950s and 1960s as long as it was given in a controlled way. (Although as many readers could doubtless testify, many times physical punishment was meted out by an adult who showed less than perfect self-control.) 'Spare the rod and spoil the child' was an acceptable tenet of child-rearing, just as capital punishment was still the ultimate deterrent in Australia as late as 1967.

Many of our social values and beliefs have changed dramatically in the last thirty or so years. In 1967, I was taught by a female teacher who received less pay than her male counterparts. Aborigines had just been included on the census and Australia still played sport against South Africa despite its discriminatory apartheid regime. We lived in an era of social inequality where men were paid more than women, some races were significantly advantaged over others and certainly had more rights, minority groups such as gays had little legitimate power and children were subservient to adults. If kids weren't subservient in a social sense then why were they allowed to be physically punished?

We now live in an era of social equality. Women have equal rights with men, which is reflected not merely through equal pay but through entry to clubs and associations that were once male-only organisations. Women are now entering the boardroom where in the past they were not made welcome. Racial discrimination has been legislated against and minority groups such as gays have gained a strong voice.

The notion of social equality extends to children, where there is an expectation that they be accorded the same social rights as adults. This is not to say that adults are not wiser, stronger or better informed than children. Rather, it implies that children have the same fundamental right to fair treatment as adults. Most people would agree that it is not appropriate to physically harm another adult, whether it is a colleague, spouse or friend. Yet it is strange how many people don't extend the same courtesy or rights to fair treatment to children. Smacking and other forms of physical punishment are out of step with our current social practices and our values.

TO SMACK OR NOT TO SMACK

You need to make up your mind as a mother or father whether you will smack or not. I strongly advocate the latter. I know parents who argue that smacking is okay for certain behaviours and at certain times. They claim that it may be okay to smack a three-year-old when they are cheeky or a tiny tot who wriggles around on the change table making nappy changing difficult, but that it is not okay to smack in other circumstances. Just as you can't be a little bit pregnant, as a parent you can't have it both ways.

Some parents claim that just a little smack is okay; it is over quickly and you can move on. The trouble with smacking is that it is usually done when a parent is annoyed or angry – it is never done in a dispassionate way. It is always fuelled by emotional intensity. It is an act of violence whichever way you want to look at it.

Parents who are leaders don't always do what they feel like. They control their emotions and refuse to hit or smack. That is how we relate to our friends and other adults – when their behaviour gets up our nose we don't hit them. We may sulk, criticise them behind their backs or just leave them off our Christmas card list but in a civilised society we don't walk in, knock on the door and bop our neighbour on the nose because they did something to annoy us. The same right to fair and reasonable treatment that maintains human dignity needs to be extended to our kids. Any time you feel like lashing out and giving your child a wallop – don't. Take a walk, move away, talk to someone, phone someone up. Do something else. Each time you show such control in the face of difficult behaviour you enjoy a personal victory.

Do yourself and your kids a favour and make the decision not to smack your children.

KIDS HAVE A VOICE

The notion of social equality complicates parenting. Children have a greater voice and increasingly like to be heard. Adulthood per se no longer assures parents compliance from children, and it certainly doesn't guarantee respect. Parents who demand compliance from children often discover that parenting is one big battle for power as they fight over every little issue. The notion of cooperation has changed. Once it referred to children as 'doing as they are told'. It is now based on mutual respect and depends on a good relationship, as it requires give and take on both sides. This is quite a paradigm shift for a hard-line authoritarian.

DISCIPLINE IS ABOUT LEARNING, NOT CONTROL

Effective discipline, as distinct from punishment, helps children to take control of their behaviour and ultimately become accountable for their actions. It recognises that children of all ages make choices about how they are to behave and will adjust their behaviour according to the feedback they receive or the consequences of the behaviour.

KIDS LEARN BEST THROUGH ACTION

Parents usually have a number of options when children misbehave or act in inappropriate ways. They can use a control or compliance method, which often involves some form of punishment, or they can use the reality of the situation that places the onus on children to control their own behaviour. The former method is usually the most convenient, whereas the latter can take time and patience but is more effective in developing a sense of self-discipline in children. Let's look at a couple of examples.

Most parents have had the experience of a young child who stands up in the bath while being washed; reasonable reminders or requests to sit are ignored. It is great fun for a child to see how far he or she can push mum or dad. What options does a parent have? One option is to use a quick smack or even gentle force to gain compliance. Another option is to use real-life consequence to teach the child to adjust their behaviour. Rather than smack or wrestle with the child, a parent may ask them to sit and let them know that if they don't sit they will be removed from the bath. If the child doesn't sit down or continues to play around then quickly finish the washing and quietly remove them. The child should receive the message that when they stand or play in the bath the fun ends – mum or dad takes them out of the bath and dries them.

Few parents would disagree that the latter is preferable but it is usually time-consuming and requires self-control. Discipline that teaches rather than discipline that controls is generally more time-consuming and often needs to be repeated until the child gets the message that mum and dad really mean what they say. But it is worth the effort.

What about discipline with an older child? A friend's ten-year-old son misbehaved so badly on a school excursion that he was banned from attending the next trip. The boy's father was bitterly disappointed but stayed away from negative methods of discipline. Wisely, he didn't rush into a full-blown discussion when he first heard about his son's performance. He was extremely angry and he knew from past experiences that any discussion at that point would have ended in a yelling match. Angry parents don't do a good job communicating with kids and angry kids don't listen. So this father chose the time and the place to talk with his son.

After dinner he went into his son's bedroom, sat down and began to talk. He let his son know that he was disappointed but he refrained from criticising, embarrassing or even grounding him. He realised that this would only have added salt to the wound and it would have been his power or control rather than the reality of the situation that would have had an impact. Instead the father used this situation to teach his son to be accountable for his behaviour. He listened to his son's side of the story. His class had been watching a dance troupe perform at a concert hall and his son became bored and began to show off in front of his friends. The trouble was that there were another two hundred or so children watching and his behaviour was so disruptive that a performer stopped mid-step and asked him to leave the auditorium. The boy claimed that he had been encouraged by his friends but admitted that the responsibility for misbehaviour was his. He knew that he had options.

The father then put the responsibility back on to his son and asked: 'What will you do now?' The boy responded, 'What do you mean. I've been banned from the next excursion. Isn't that enough?'

'You interrupted an entire show. What are you going to do about that?'

The father put the responsibility of the behaviour back squarely on his son's shoulders. He turned this situation into a learning experience, not to punish him but to teach him to be accountable for his actions. 'I guess I should apologise. But how?' They talked together about different options. The boy agreed that he would write a letter to the dance troupe apologising for his behaviour. This took considerable effort, as he had to find out their address and the name of the troupe's leader. He also apologised to his teacher for his behaviour and outlined how he would behave next time.

The father continued: 'What about next time or when you are in class and your friends annoy you or encourage you to mess around? What will you do?' They discussed options such as ignoring them, sitting elsewhere or even come-back lines he may use to refuse their invitations to misbehave but keep his dignity intact. The father explored options to resolve this situation and avoid similar situations in the future.

Discipline that teaches looks forward rather than backward and is more concerned with what will happen in the future rather than what has happened in the past. It is important to discuss with children appropriate ways of behaving next time they are in similar situations. If a child whines to gain your attention, let them know how to gain your full attention next time. They may even rehearse the words that they can use.

Discipline that teaches involves the following:

1. The child is aware of his or her behaviour.
2. The child has ownership of the problem.
3. Suitable options are explored and they are discussed in more detail if applicable.
4. Both you and the child keep your dignity intact.

DISCIPLINE DOESN'T HAVE TO BE TIME-CONSUMING

I'm not suggesting that we deal with every misbehaviour in such a detailed, orderly way. That is impractical. Many behaviours need to be dealt with immediately and the language of control is the most appropriate. A mother who rushes out to work hasn't the time to sit down and discuss the pros and cons of a situation when her son answers her request to be home from school at four o'clock with 'Why?' Sometimes the language of compliance is the only way to gain the cooperation that you require. However, it may be suitable to sit down with your child later when you are less rushed and discuss the virtues of cooperation in the morning sans the mouthful of questions.

DISCIPLINE STARTS WITH YOU

Discipline involves self-control. You are the locus of control, not your children. The first person to control when children misbehave is you. When you can control yourself you have a much greater chance of influencing your child. The battle for self-control is perhaps the greatest challenge that many parents have.

Many factors influence parental self-control when children are less than perfect, including state of mind, the time the day, fatigue, lifestyle, the number of children involved and the type of behaviour. As a morning person I can react differently to misbehaviour that occurs at breakfast than a similar behaviour that occurs at night when I am tired and looking for a break. When my work piles up and the pressure grows I am more likely to snap at my children than take a conciliatory approach. And some misbehaviours trigger a stronger reaction than others. Sibling fighting of the high-pitched noisy variety makes the hairs on the back of my neck stand on end. At these times I go to another part of the house so I won't interfere (which would only add to the conflict). Anyone with two or more kids under the age of five will testify that keeping cool under pressure is a battle.

Many factors impact on our lives and make self-control difficult, but in the long-term best interests of children they need to be dealt with. If you are worn out by the daily grind of raising young children with little assistance or let-up then a break is imperative. Or if your lifestyle is so busy that you are rushing from one task to another with little chance to talk to children, let alone take the time to sort out a few problems, then it may be appropriate to make some changes to your lifestyle. Kids, regardless of their age, require a great deal of our time and energy. They also have a way of making parents stop and take notice.

Nine-year-old Jason found a rather extreme way of gaining his parents' attention. Both his parents were extremely busy. His father, Allan, was working long hours in a new business and his mother had just returned to being a full-time student. What little time and energy his parents had seemed to be directed toward Jason's older brother, who was having difficulty settling into secondary school. Realising that he had neglected his family, Allan decided to take his two sons away for a weekend of fishing. While packing for the big weekend, Allan saw Jason's name etched into the roof of the car. Showing enormous restraint, he chose to ignore it for the moment rather than spoil the weekend. After the trip, Allan and his wife sat with Jason and asked him about writing his name on the car roof. Jason came clean immediately and admitted fault. He then unleashed a tale of woe letting his parents know about his academic problems, friendship difficulties and also about some bullying that he was receiving at school. For the first time in many months, Jason had his parents' undivided attention and he was going to make the most of the opportunity. His parents realised that they hadn't attended to their son in a while and that vandalism was one way to gain their attention. That afternoon they put some changes into place that would ensure that Jason wouldn't feel so neglected again.

FOCUS ON YOU

Often our instinctive reactions to children encourage their misbehaviour to continue. Maurice Balson in *Becoming Better Parents* (p. 16) makes the following claim:

> As all human behaviour has a purpose, the key to understanding and correcting a child's behaviour is to identify the purpose and then act in such a way that the behaviour does not achieve its intended goal.

This is an unconventional but sensible way of viewing human behaviour. Children don't act in a vacuum. Most of their actions have some sort of purpose or pay-off, otherwise they would desist. Children are adept at working out the behaviours that provide them with a pay-off with one parent and those that provide no response whatsoever. My first two children decided very early in life not to come to my side of the bed when they woke up at night. My wife was far more likely to wake up and provide them with the comfort they wanted. However, because my wife had gone back to work, my youngest child learned that I was the one who was more amenable at night, so she would bypass her mother to come to me.

The same principle was at work when my eldest son, Sam, decided to have some fun when he was put to bed as a toddler. No sooner did we put him to bed than he would be back out in the living room – just like a boomerang he would return. Our first response was to ask him to go back to his room. When this invariably failed we would coax him, persuade him and eventually yell at him to return to his room. He pushed us precisely to the point where we were about to lose our cool, then he would desist. Sam had found a terrific way to keep us busy with him.

To change our young boomerang's behaviour so that he remained in his room and kept himself occupied until he fell asleep, it was first necessary to change our own behaviour. No more reminding, coaxing or urging when he came out of his room; our impulsive reactions gave him just the feedback he required. We had two options: either completely ignore him or return him in silence to his room whenever he came out. Fortunately, the first option was successful but it took a great deal of self-control to ignore his requests for a drink, a kiss or a hug. (He was given more than his ample share of affection before bedtime.) It was an amusing scene the first time that we decided to ignore him. Sam called out for a drink, a hug or one more kiss like he normally did – anything to gain our attention. When this behaviour didn't work, he came out of his room to talk to us. Although he was extremely persistent, we continued to act as if he wasn't there. We even ignored him when he sat between us and the television set. As it was no fun being with the adults if they completely ignored him, he eventually became bored and returned to his bedroom. The boomerang's behaviour was changed in one rather long night because we changed our own way of responding and stopped providing him with the feedback that fuelled his behaviour.

It is important to note that this method may not be suitable for all children. Sam wasn't likely to run outside or do anything destructive if he was ignored. This example simply illustrates the principle of changing your own behaviour to bring about a change in that of your child. You may have to adapt it to suit your own circumstances.

Parents often ask me how they can prevent an adolescent from arguing with them every time they make a request or ask for some cooperation. The simple answer is that they can't but they can refuse to argue with a teenager. Repeat a request or leave the room when a teenager begins an argument. Kids will eventually learn that it is pointless answering back, as they don't get any response. Of course, it takes longer for some for the message to sink in. This may mean that parents check their own posture and body language when making a request. Often the way parents ask will determine the cooperation they receive, and sometimes the behaviour will intensify before it reduces. So often the volume level raises or the comments become personal when parents refuse to enter an argument with a young person.

This principle of changing your own behaviour to achieve a change in the behaviour of others is a powerful way of influencing people. Many parents who are frustrated because they have little control over their children can take comfort in the fact that they can control their own behaviours and so influence, rather than coerce, the behaviours of the children they interact with. It also recognises the fact that children are responsible for their own behaviours but they are also influenced by the reactions of those around them.

THINK BEFORE YOU ACT

For many parents, effective discipline requires you to change the way you typically react when children misbehave. If you are an impulsive type of person it may take some effort to catch yourself before you deliver a mouthful of criticism, bark a series of orders, or nag your child to do the right thing. If you are a parent of an adolescent, no doubt you have learned that the only thing you can be spontaneous about is your affection. It is best to keep a tight guard on what you do and say with this age group.

PARENTING WITH FIRMNESS

One day I dropped into a friend's place unexpectedly and was invited to stay for a meal. I took up the invitation and was looking forward to catching up on what my friend had been doing. I was to be disappointed. Our dinner conversation was marred by my friend's four-year-old daughter who sat on both her parents' knees at different times before sitting on mine. When she wasn't asking incessant questions she was deliberately dropping food on the floor. It was quite obvious that this type of behaviour was commonplace and her parents did little to stop her. In short, few limits were placed on this child to teach her about appropriate behaviour.

Limits and rules

Limits and rules that establish a framework for appropriate behaviour usually involve space (play in this place), time (be home by dinnertime) or explanations about how behaviour should occur (put petrol in the car before you give me back the keys). They help children to become socialised and even likeable.

Kids like limits and rules; they make them feel safe and secure. But they will also push against limits and will often see if we are serious or not. Parents and teachers need to hold the line when kids push the limits. A friend told an amusing story about how his thirteen-year-old son pushed the limits that he had imposed.

The father took his son to the video store to choose a video – dad's shout. The boy went straight to the adult section and chose an M-rated movie, much to his father's disapproval; the father followed the government censor's word to the letter and wouldn't allow his son to watch M-rated movies until he was fifteen, the recommended age. The son didn't take his father's decision lying down. He decided to push the limits in a public place using some well-chosen lines. 'It's not fair. You never let me have any fun. Besides, all the other kids at school have seen this.' He brought out the heavy artillery – an appeal to fairness and some emotional blackmail for making him feel like the odd person out with his peer group. This father continued to hold firm.

But this young teenager wasn't about to let his father off so lightly. He refused his invitation to borrow another video and sat in the car while his father chose his own. The teenager continued the emotional blackmail by sulking all the way home. The father admitted that the sulking (silent temper tantrum) nearly worked in terms of making him change his mind. He almost relented and turned back to rent his son the M-rated video but held firm.

Like many toddlers, emergent teenagers often turn limit-pushing into an art form. Of course, sometimes such less than gentle prodding is a sign that the rules are inapplicable or it is time to sit down and negotiate some new boundaries. Perhaps in this case it might have been suitable for the father to agree to his son's request and that they sit down and watch the movie together.

Who works out what?

Up until the 1960s there was little doubt who imposed most of the limits on children in our culture – adults. 'Kids should be seen but not heard' was a popular maxim. Parenting was relatively simple in the days when kids were kids and everyone knew their place. The social revolution of the 1960s resulted in greater freedom of choice being given to individuals and authority of all types was brought into question. Traditional autocratic child-raising methods based around reward and punishment were replaced by a more permissive approach that gave children a great deal of freedom with fewer restrictions on their behaviour. This method of child-rearing is questionable to say the least, as the socialisation process requires that children learn to live and work with others. Limits and rules make this possible. The democratic approach to raising children that became popular in the 1980s was a type of compromise between both approaches. The democratic or authoritative approach involves parents and children working at setting limits and rules together. This approach reflects current popular social practice and is my preferred method of raising children, but it should not be the only way. It is also a greatly misunderstood method of raising children. (See figures 2 and 3.)

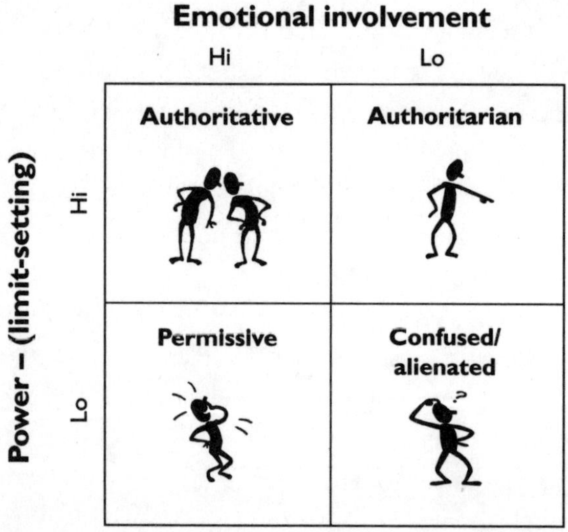

Emotional involvement

	Hi	Lo
Hi	Authoritative	Authoritarian
Lo	Permissive	Confused/ alienated

Power – (limit-setting)

Figure 2: Parent-child relationships.

When working out who sets rules and limits it is necessary to consider the age and personalities of children, the specific situations involved and your own parenting style. Flexibility is the key and intuition is important. Parents who follow a single approach such as the democratic approach will invariably find that it has its limitations. For instance, it is impractical to negotiate with a toddler and time-consuming to discuss every issue with a teenager. An autocratic parent may find that a child who meekly consented to the parent's wishes is not quite so amenable when he or she reaches adolescence.

There are times when parents set limits and rules with children's and their own best interests in mind. The 'parents rule' approach is most suitable when children are very young and need rules set for them. Regardless of the age of the children, there are situations and times when parents need compliance and have little time or inclination to get into a protracted discussion. For instance, 'Be home straight away after school' is a reasonable request, which is not up for discussion when I am leaving the house in the morning.

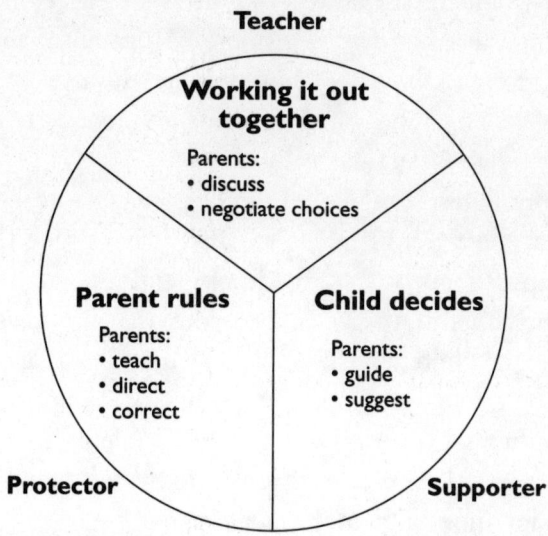

Figure 3: Authoritative parenting – 'guided democracy'.

Parents and children can work many rules and behavioural limits out as children develop the skills to participate in joint decision-making. This approach is time-consuming but it is worth the effort. It is almost mandatory if you have an adolescent who wants an increasing amount of freedom, so it is best to brush up on your negotiating skills if you have an emergent teenager in the family. It is also effective if you want to give the children input into the organisation of family life.

There are times when parents stay out of children's lives and allow them the freedom to choose and safely experience the consequences of their decisions. Children's choice of clothing and eating habits are two areas where many wise parents refuse to interfere.

Different approaches for different children

Different children within a family prefer different approaches. My youngest child, Sarah, prefers to have limits imposed on her rather than participate in the decision-making process, or even at times make decisions for herself. She will happily be told what time she should be home from a friend's place, what she should wear and exactly when she should unpack her bag. She likes the security of having her environment structured by others and needs a great deal of prompting to make her own decisions. For instance, an invitation to contribute ideas on how we should share the use of the family computer will be met by a shrug of the shoulders as if to say 'I'm happy to abide by your decision'.

However, my eldest daughter, Emma, prefers to make her own decisions about most things in life and will often argue the point if limits are imposed. Bedtimes, bedroom tidiness and choice of clothing can be contentious issues if we impose our views unwisely. She is the type of child who likes to feel that she is in control so participation in decision-making, even if illusory, is important to her.

My son Sam who is a young teenager is flexible in his approach to decision-making. He is also at a stage where increasingly he is taking responsibility for more and more areas of his life. For instance, he makes his own decisions about bedtime and get-up time in the morning. The issue of going out at night is a joint decision and issues such as permission to go out and home time are usually negotiated.

There are times when children may appreciate a different approach to limit-setting. Sam, who enjoys quite a bit of freedom to decide within limits, found the experience of starting secondary school overwhelming. Being at the bottom of the pecking order where he was unsure of the rules of the playground was just one challenge he had to meet. Making new friends, adjusting to new teachers, changing classrooms for each subject and learning to work to a timetable were some of the adjustments he had to make. Some kids take these new experiences in their stride but it is natural for them to experience some difficulty making the transition from primary to secondary school.

Sam wasn't coping all that well with the new experiences so we structured his environment at home and made most of his daily decisions for him, dictating when he should get up, when he should leave, when he should come home and what type of lunch to take. For a few weeks he was happy to have these decisions made for him. As he grew accustomed to his new experiences we gradually gave him control of these areas of his life.

A sense of security

Limits provide children with a sense of security. Children like to know that they exist and they also like to break them. Children up to the age of eight solve most of their social problems using rules. You may have heard young children talk in terms of 'I am not allowed to do that', 'My mum said that you shouldn't throw things at others' or 'The teacher said we should ...' Watch any group of school children playing a game and you can be sure that they are following a set of rules. If there are no rules then children will generally construct their own. Even preschool-aged children will often establish a loose set of rules to govern their free play.

Sometimes children will go to great lengths to test the limits and can be reassured to find they exist. One three-year-old who lived in a household that contained few limits found a unique way of becoming accustomed to the structured environment of three-year-old preschool. His home environment was chaotic as there were few restrictions placed on his behaviour or that of his siblings. When he came to kindergarten once a week he would always do something dangerous such as throw a block, tip over a toy, or even hurt a child. He would never repeat the behaviour. The preschool teacher would be ready for James when he behaved in such a way. She would quietly go to him and inform him that the behaviour was unacceptable and then redirect his attention to an enjoyable activity. James was unconsciously testing the waters every time he came into the structured environment of preschool. Reassured that his environment was safe and secure, James would not repeat his testing behaviours.

KEEPING THE END IN MIND

Discipline is by far the hardest and at times most confusing part of raising children. An aim of effective parenting is to develop a sense of self-discipline whereby children regulate their own behaviour and make their own decisions. Children need practice at making decisions for themselves so parents who keep this end in mind will provide children with the opportunities to determine their own behaviours. Invariably, children will sometimes fall flat on their faces and be hurt. But there are also times when kids need to have limits imposed by parents stepping in and holding the line because it is in their children's long-term best interests for them to do so. It takes a wise parent to know the difference. But that is what leadership is about.

4

SIBLING RIVALRY – HELPING CHILDREN MANAGE CONFLICT

*The measure of a healthy family is how strongly kids
pull together when the chips are down.*

Anonymous

Sibling fighting is an entrenched part of family life. If your children argue and squabble with each other then welcome to the human race. All the evidence suggests that you and your family are normal. Yes, fighting is annoying for parents. Yes, kids can be cruel to each other with their comments and actions. Yes, it happens far more frequently than most parents would like. But sibling fighting has its benefits for families as a group and for children.

Let's look at the benefits for individuals. It would be great to think that children would always live in harmony and always see eye to eye. But whenever a group of people live in close proximity for an extended period of time there is bound to be conflict. When those people happen to be children perhaps as young as two, who lack the skills to resolve conflicts in a relatively civil manner then there is bound to be acrimony.

Children have two choices when conflict occurs – either they deal with it and work it out or they avoid it. Avoidance of conflict is okay sometimes. It is wiser for a child who has a homework deadline pending to ignore an annoying sibling than become embroiled in a time-consuming argument. However, those children who continuously avoid conflict don't learn how to handle themselves in conflict situations outside their family home. Many children who are the victims of bullying haven't learned to stick up for themselves in the relatively safe confines of the family home. Conversely, many schoolyard bullies have been bullied themselves by a sibling, so conflict needs adult intervention.

The family home is a good place for children to develop the skills of assertion and learn to stick up for themselves. However, kids will often use the skills of aggression, so parents need to step in sometimes and make sure kids stick to the rules of fair fighting. Kids who avoid fighting at home will often turn into passive adults who avoid conflict at all costs. As spouses they walk away from conflict rather than deal with it directly and in the workplace they fail to stick up for their point of view or seek a negotiated solution when problems occur.

MODELLING

Modelling appropriate strategies is one way to teach children to handle conflict. Children will invariably look to their same-sex parents for clues about resolving differences with others. If you shout each time you are locked in conflict with another person, don't be surprised if your child lifts the roof and yells at force-ten gale proportions whenever she or he is inconvenienced. If you are into hurling objects across the kitchen when things don't go your way then it should come as no surprise if teachers report that textbook throwing is part of your child's repertoire of behaviours in the classroom. If sulking is more your bag then you had better buy your child a supply of dolls and pins so that he or she can place pins in replicas of real people when sulking in the bedroom. If you hit then they will hit. Of course, children can pick up inappropriate ways of resolving issues from other sources such as the television or their peers, but none of these are as significant sources as their parents.

We all lose our cool from time to time; to suggest that adults always handle their differences in a civil manner would be to place them on pedestals. We get tired or the adrenalin pumps and before we realise it we have blurted a mouthful of venom at a partner or child: 'You rotten little so-and so. You've left my hammer outside and now I can't find it. You are so irresponsible. Or are you stupid, plain stupid?' Such an example is a model that you would rather a child didn't copy. As a leader, you should apologise to a child who may have been on the receiving end of such a verbal barrage. 'Oops. Sorry about that. It was over the top. I am really annoyed about my hammer but that doesn't give me the right to fly off like that. I didn't mean the insults.' Kids need to see you apologise and know that if they lose their tempers they too can apologise and try again.

WHEN AND HOW TO INTERFERE

Families and children will invariably handle conflict with varying degrees of skill and effectiveness. Parents who are effective leaders won't avoid family fighting but look for opportunities to help children deal with it constructively. They won't always interfere in disputes as children have an uncanny knack of working out their own solutions. A while ago my two eldest children, both in the prime of their prepubescent lives, had been waging an ongoing war for some time. The issues they argued over were relatively minor – choice of television viewing, chores, and who said what to whom.

As they rarely resort to physical combat and they both give as much as they receive in the area of verbal warfare, I generally give them the opportunity to work out their differences. One time when I decided to enter the fray to help broker a peace resolution they chorused 'We nearly had it worked out then you interfered, Dad.' They had a valid point, but there are times when parents need to step in and offer some help, even if it is only to remind them that, despite the public actions of some of our politicians, intimidation and personal insults should not be part of the conflict resolution process. It is worth reinforcing these views without becoming too upset if children don't always follow the advice given.

Kids usually are adept at involving parents in their disputes. They may come to you with tales of near murder and mayhem inflicted by one sibling on a hapless victim; alternatively, noise becomes so great or the behaviour so upsetting that it is impossible to stay out. Most research suggests that when kids are given the opportunity they are generally able to resolve their disputes equitably over time. When we interfere to punish one for starting an argument or fight then the conflict may settle in the short term but it will often only flare up later due to resentment or because the dispute hasn't been fully resolved.

Sometimes the best approach for a parent is to stay out and allow a dispute or argument to take its course, even if the methods kids use may not come straight from the guidelines laid down by the Geneva Convention. If there is no imbalance of power then it may be appropriate to:

- bear the dispute (if you are able to ignore the noisy squabbles)
- beat it (move away from the warring parties so that your peace is not disturbed)
- boot them out (invite them to settle their differences in another area of the home or even outside).

Helping them work out a solution

By focusing on the issue that children or young people are arguing about, parents can become involved in useful ways that teach them to resolve problems amicably without resorting to name-calling, insults and physical means. Most kids don't want parents to help out in this manner. They generally want parents to punish the other child or to make some type of ruling in their favour.

By focusing on the problem at hand and offering suggestions to break an impasse or reach some type of agreement, parents are being constructive rather than merely being arbiters in a dispute.

Clearing the air

In families, disagreements happen that parents just can't stop. Siblings, particularly teenagers of the opposite sex, can tease and be downright cruel to each other. Despite the best of parental intentions and positive modelling, young people have been known to spit out venomous insults at a rapid-fire pace without caring who gets hurt.

This type of verbal sparring or sniping between siblings occurs for a multitude of reasons and can be extremely difficult for the rest of the family to listen to. One idea is to provide children with an opportunity to clear the air and get their feelings out in the open. Such an approach can be hurtful but often it gets to the heart of the matter and allows them both to move on. Parents who use this method need to be firm, neutral and not easily shocked.

STEVE, PHILIP AND JESSICA

Steve was on a family holiday with his wife and three children. His two eldest, Philip, aged 14, and Jessica, aged 12, had spent the first week of the break practically at each other's throats. Steve had tried ignoring them but the intensity and frequency of their verbal jousting was increasing so he thought that it was time his children cleared the air.

He invited them to sit opposite each other in the family caravan and told them what he had witnessed between the two over the past week or so. He was careful not to accuse one of initiating the sniping and he made sure he stuck to the facts. He spoke about what he had observed and heard. 'Philip, this is what I see, I may be wrong from your point of view, but this is what I have been seeing and hearing lately. Every time your sister says anything at all you jump down her throat and criticise her. It seems she only has to open her mouth and you are critical or insulting towards her.'

'Jessica, everything your brother does is criticised. Nothing he does is good enough for you. It also seems that you play with your young sister and deliberately leave your brother out of the conversation.'

'Yeah, but Philip deserves it. He is always mean to me.'

'Jessica, I am only telling you what I see.'

'Philip, is there anything you'd like to say to your sister? I am not talking about apologising.'

Philip let fly, 'Yeah, you just get on my nerves. You think you are just so good at everything.'

'Yeah, but Philip. I don't do anything and you just criticise me.'

Then with tears in his eyes Philip blurted out, 'Jess, you are good at all the cool things – sport, schoolwork, everything. The only thing I am good at is art, and no-one cares about that. It's not fair. I hate you for being good.'

Steve quietly broke the silence that followed, 'Okay so we have found out how you are feeling Philip. Pretty down, it seems, about a number of things. You and I can talk about that later. In the meantime, I want you to tell each other one thing that you want the other to do. Jessica, you first.

'Okay. Philip, I just want you to stop yelling at me and disagreeing with me all the time. It gets so I don't want to speak to anyone when you're around anymore.'

'Jess, stop laughing at my new hairstyle. I know you do. I hate that.'

'You have heard what each other asked. Do we have some commitment here kids?' said Steve. Both agreed and left feeling emotionally exhausted. Steve made a note to talk to Philip later about his revelations to his sister. He obviously needed someone to talk this over with.

Teach them how to fight fairly

Kids don't always fight fairly and stick to the rules. Anecdotal evidence strongly suggests that they will criticise each other, hit each other, yell at each other and throw tantrums to get their own way. They will also whinge, whine, swear, make rude gestures and generally pick on each other. Preschool-aged kids, particularly boys, are prone to hitting, smacking or even pinching when there is a dispute. Adolescent girls are known to flick sarcastic barbs at each other with particular reference to appearance, body shape or even boy stuff.

Brave parents need to stick their noses in somehow and reinforce to kids that there needs to be some fairness, or a set of rules that they should follow when there is conflict. It is important to be aware that kids may not necessarily follow your advice but should be reminded of it anyway. Somewhere, sometime down the track when they are older, perhaps as adults, they will recall your message and most probably tell it to their own children. Some messages are worth repeating and the important messages have a habit of sticking for life.

Some reasonable rules for disputes to reinforce are:

- Stick to the point when arguing.
- Avoid personal insults – no put-downs.
- No hitting or physical contact unless, of course, you are giving a sibling a hug.

NO PUT-DOWNS PLEASE

Make an effort to eliminate the use of put-downs in your family. This means that negative comments about weight, body shape, appearance, religion, gender and other personal derogatory remarks designed to insult or put someone down are off-limits.

This can be relatively easy to enforce when children are preschool or school-aged, but difficult when adolescents are bigger than you and their tongues have been sharpened by years of schoolyard repartee, but put-downs are worth getting assertive over. When put-downs are used, raise to your full height if needed, make solid eye contact and calmly let the person hurling the put-downs know that such comments are not welcome in your family. Be firm and insistent. Be strong. Put-downs are insidious and destroy the feeling of psychological safety that needs to exist in a family. Your children should at least feel that someone is supporting them even if the behaviour continues behind your back.

MY CHILD IS ALWAYS BEING PICKED ON

Often one child in a family appears to be teased or 'picked on' more than others. Such a situation is naturally quite worrying for parents.

As odd as it may seem, the victim can have a vested interest in being picked on and will intentionally or unintentionally continue behaviours that invite victimisation. Sometimes kids who appear to be victimised do a fine job of annoying siblings to the point that they end up being hit or verbally abused. For some kids it is satisfying to know that mum or dad is on their side when they go to them with their tales. The pay-off in terms of extra attention can be enormous in some cases.

Teach kids some coping skills

Teach children some conflict avoidance skills so that they have an alternative to becoming involved in a dispute. Younger children should be able to go to the safety of a bedroom or some other safe place within your home to avoid a situation of conflict. It is helpful to point out any behaviours that may inadvertently contribute to teasing and replace them with positive behaviours. Older children and adolescents can use rehearsed comeback lines to deflect verbal criticism. Lines such as 'Thanks very much for your opinion but I happen to think otherwise' are more effective comebacks to personal criticism than a whine or an insult, which is standard fare for many kids.

Part 2

GIVING THEM TOOLS FOR LIFE

I heard fellow parent educator Jeanette Acland tell a wonderful story in one of her seminars, one that every parent should hear.* She tells of the son of a wealthy merchant who, impatient to receive his inheritance, asked his father for his share immediately. The merchant, although hurt and disappointed, agreed to his son's request. Taking his inheritance, the young man said goodbye to his father and headed to the city. He had lived a sheltered life so he was very naive about the ways of the world, which made him fair prey for every conman who could spot a sucker a mile away. Being young and headstrong, he refused to take advice from anyone, least of all his father. Like many young people he was convinced that he knew it all.

At first he really enjoyed life. He lived in the best hotels, ate in the finest restaurants and wore fashionable clothes. With that sort of lifestyle it was not surprising that women were attracted to him like bees to a honey pot. Life was sweet. However, the good times didn't last long. He quickly squandered his wealth on both his pursuit of the good life and a series of get-rich-quick schemes.

With his fortune gone and with few job prospects, he found himself homeless, friendless and with little apparent future. As he sat huddled under a bridge feeling hungry and cold he looked once more in the kitbag that his father had given him to see if there were any coins tucked away. As he picked at the seams he found humility. He continued to look and he found the inner strength to go on another day. He kept looking and kept uncovering more treasures – he found forgiveness, honesty, integrity and self-respect. Where did all these qualities and strengths come from? Suddenly he realised that it was his father who had put them there. His father had given him what he really needed to make his way in the world. His father had been cultivating these qualities all his life but he didn't know it at the time, although they were there when they were really needed.

The son got up from the gutter and made his way home. He was poor but he was strong; he had left home a child and returned a man.

---

* Jeanette's version of this story is contained in her collection titled *Whole Parish Parenting*, Anglican Diocese of Melbourne, 1998.

Ecstatic that his son had returned, the merchant arranged a huge party to welcome him.

When I heard this wonderful story for the first time I began to think about my own parenting in a different way and question the real contribution that I would make for my kids. I began to think about the qualities and values that I was developing in my own children. What was I putting in their kitbag that they could draw on as adults? What tools was I helping them develop that would enable them to stand on their own two feet when they were on their own? What strengths, values and resources could they draw on when they had difficulties, as they invariably would? I began to think about the lasting legacies that I was leaving my children that transcend the managerial aspects of parenting.

This part discusses the life skills that we promote for our children. It looks at developing a sense of optimism, promoting a sense of competency, developing the skills of emotional literacy and developing of a number of key values that children can place in their kitbags for life.

5

BUILDING OPTIMISM IN CHILDREN

There is no sadder sight than a young pessimist.

MARK TWAIN

The terms optimism and pessimism have gained enormous currency in recent years and I suspect that they have lost much of their real meaning. The popular view of an optimist is that of a person who sees the bright side of life and always looks for the good in people and events. Perhaps the fellow hanging on the cross in the Monty Python movie *The Life of Brian* singing 'Always Look on the Bright Side of Life' is the ultimate optimist. Cynics would suggest that anyone facing death by crucifixion had no choice but to look on the bright side. And there is the now-familiar analogy of the optimist viewing a glass as half full of liquid and the pessimist describing the glass as half empty.

Optimism is more than just looking on the bright side or seeing the glass as half full. It is more than just viewing the world through rose-coloured glasses or always searching for that silver lining. To dismiss optimism as simple 'boosterism' is to neglect the powerful impact that it has on our mental state, our physical health and our ability to succeed in work and relationships and to achieve our full potential. Optimism is an entrenched habit of mind that impacts on all areas of a person's life.

THE IMPACT OF PESSIMISM

Martin Seligman, through his groundbreaking work on optimism and pessimism, chronicles the disastrous impact of pessimism in the United States. He maintains that his homeland is experiencing an unprecedented epidemic of pessimism that is having disastrous effects on the physical and emotional well-being of Americans. According to Seligman's significant research, pessimists experience more depression and achieve less in school, the workplace and other fields of endeavour such as sport than optimists. Their physical health is worse than that of optimists. It is easy to dismiss Seligman's work as crackpot or as an example of another new age view of the world, but Seligman's research involves half a million people over twenty years. His work is important and should be listened to by every parent, every teacher and every professional who works with young people.

Pessimism is fast becoming a trendy way of looking at the world that children and young people are absorbing. It involves looking at negative aspects of events and leads to underachievement, lack of effort and resignation. It is also a self-fulfilling prophecy, as each setback or disappointment that a person experiences reinforces their pessimistic view of the world. It can be mistaken for mere cynicism but it is more sinister than that. It has a number of guises, including the popular posture among young males that it is 'cool to be a fool'. Criticising themselves, each other, figures of authority and even institutions such as schools is now one of the most popular games around for the cynical adolescent. The tragedy of cynicism is that it provides a person with a terrific excuse not to put in the effort to create anything or improve a situation he or she is in. Cynicism leads to apathy, which is the natural ally of pessimism. Pessimism undermines trying, as it divests a person of responsibility and allows the cycles of failure and depression to occur. Pessimistic beliefs tend to be self-fulfilling prophecies which in turn confirm a person's original beliefs about him or herself.

THE FOLLY OF THE SELF-ESTEEM ETHIC

During the 1970s and 1980s a strange thing happened in homes and schools across Australia. The prime child-rearing message in this period was that a healthy self-esteem was central to a child's development. A child's learning and happiness were linked to a healthy level of self-esteem. So parents and teachers went to great lengths to make children feel better about themselves. Praise became the main tool to achieve a high level of self-esteem, so children grew used to hearing positive things said about them. 'You're terrific!' 'Good girl' and other platitudes became *de rigueur* for every well-meaning parent and teacher across the country. The trouble is that when praise isn't linked to achievement it becomes meaningless patter.

In an effort to make children feel good about themselves we avoided exposing kids to experiences of failure. As a result, students in schools no longer failed; rather, their performance was measured according to a set of development markers. 'He is not ready to learn those skills yet' or 'Her skills are still developing' have become a catchcry in many Australian schools. To an extent we have failed to adequately challenge kids, as we haven't allowed them to consider failure as an option; nor have we allowed them to experience the frustration that comes from grappling to learn a difficult skill, whether it is a four-year-old learning to tie their shoelaces or a thirteen-year-old coming to grips with some difficult maths concepts.

How do children know that they have really succeeded unless they have avoided failing or have overcome challenges? I don't recommend that constant failure is good for kids; on the contrary, continued experiences of failure can be detrimental to a child developing a healthy self-esteem. Let's face it, most adults give up or avoid activities where they constantly fail in order to protect their self-esteem. But experiences of failure help children experience the thrill and satisfaction of succeeding. There is no better way to boost your self-esteem than to overcome hardships or succeed in the face of difficulty. Failure and success are natural allies.

In an effort to help kids feel good about themselves, we have tried to shield them not only from failure but from feeling sad, disappointed and anxious. I am not suggesting that we purposefully allow kids to feel bad or promote sadness, disappointment and anxiety as permanent states, but these negative feelings all have a purpose and we shouldn't try to hide children from them or move children on if they are feeling bad. Anxiety, sadness and anger invariably involve personal pain but they are also the first lines of defence against danger, loss and trespass.

Unfortunately, we forgot that self-esteem as a feeling needs to come from doing. In order to feel good, kids must do well by overcoming challenges and experiencing a sense of mastery. Self-esteem is firmly grounded in mastery and competence. Without mastery as the base then self-esteem building is pure boosterism. Words not supported by deeds then become meaningless.

Persistence and overcoming frustration have their place in building self-esteem. We will go to great lengths to do things for kids because it is easier or because we don't want them to experience frustration. But whether kids are learning to tie shoelaces or learning a difficult maths concept at school, by stepping back we provide them with an opportunity to gain mastery and the true sense of self-esteem that comes through accomplishment and overcoming challenge and obstacles. As parents, we can encourage children's efforts and praise their persistence but our language is only a tool to help children attain. It is the achievement rather than the words of praise or encouragement themselves that helps children and young people feel good about themselves.

WHAT'S OPTIMISM ABOUT?

The common view of optimism is that it is a positive or upbeat view of the world. Optimists look on the flip side of negative events for some good, some hope and some reason to be positive. Visualisation of success and the use of affirmative, positive language are generally considered the stock tools of trade for today's garden-variety optimists. But such positivism is only one part of optimism. According to Seligman, the basis for optimism is in the way that a person thinks about causes of events rather than positive language or positive visualisation. In particular, whether a person views an event as permanent or temporary, who is to blame and how much of their life are affected by an event indicates whether a person is an optimist or a pessimist. Everyone has an explanatory style that they use to explain negative or positive events. Pessimists explain events differently than optimists, which reflects their beliefs about the causes of negative or positive events. These explanations involve permanence, pervasiveness and personalising blame.

Pessimists tend to do the following:

- explain negative events as permanent rather than temporary: 'I can't get a job because the economy stinks.' (Belief: The situation will persist despite any effort I make.)
- personalise blame: 'I can't fix the car because I am no good with my hands.' (Belief: I am at fault.)
- catastrophise about the effects of the event: 'My kids are the worst kids in the street.' (Belief: I am hard done by. It is not fair.)

Optimists, on the other hand, explain negative events using different criteria. Optimists tend to do the following:

- see negative events as temporary: 'I can't get a job because my interview skills are letting me down.' (Belief: I can improve my chances of getting a job by working on my skills.)
- rationalise blame: 'I can't fix the car because I don't know enough about mechanics.' (Belief: I can do something about it if I want.)
- look at specific events, rather than take a global view: 'My kids are pretty hard to deal with around bedtime.' (Belief: They are okay the rest of the time so I can enjoy being with them.)

The result of optimists' explanatory styles is that they reflect the belief that something can be done about negative events. In each example, the optimist puts themself in a position to alleviate or improve the difficult situation. The pessimist's explanatory style offers an excuse in each case not to do anything. Pessimists believe that negative events are out of their control, which offers a perfect excuse not to change. Optimists operate under a belief system that they can control events and thus affect outcomes or at least turn outcomes around to suit them. Consequently, optimism is a powerful position for children and adults to adopt – one that encourages them to act in the face of difficulties.

Similarly, optimists and pessimists explain positive events differently. Optimists believe that good events have permanent causes and are likely to happen again, whereas pessimists believe positive events occur by chance or when conditions are in their favour.

An optimist thinks, 'I passed the test because I am clever and I worked hard', whereas a pessimist thinks, 'I passed the test because the questions were easy. That was lucky.' Kids who believe that their success has permanent causes will be more likely to work hard at school or in any area of endeavour because they believe that they can affect the results. On the other hand, kids who look for temporary causes may give up even when they do well, thinking that success was a matter of chance or a fluke.

Optimists explain positive events in terms of global reasons and pessimists generally provide a narrow, specific cause for their success. An optimist believes 'Ali invited me to her birthday party because I am popular.' A pessimist believes 'Ali invited me to her party because she feels sorry for me.' Both explanations may be true, but the explanatory style reveals a great deal about each person's view of himself or herself. The first view shows the belief that success (in this case in the area of making friends) lies with the child and the second view places the responsibility or control with the other person. Seligman found that those children who think about good events in terms of global causes performed better across more walks of life than those who explained their success in narrow specific terms.

WHERE DO KIDS GAIN THEIR OPTIMISTIC OR PESSIMISTIC VIEWS?

Pessimism is not inborn. While some children may be predisposed to pessimism due to their genetic make-up, it is more a product of social conditioning. It is a view of reality that children learn from the significant adults in their lives, including parents and teachers.

The media, with its penchant for taking a negative or cynical position about most events from politics to current affairs, helps peddle pessimism in young people.

Seligman maintains that children construct their optimistic or pessimistic views of the world and events by the age of eight. A number of factors lead to the development of pessimism or optimism in children. A child's early experience of success or failure is one factor. The foundations of optimism are laid when a child develops a notion that she or he is competent, which is constructed through successful interactions with the world. The foundations for pessimism are laid when children constantly meet failure rather than success or are deprived of opportunities to do things for themselves. Chapter 6 looks at ways parents can help children to develop a sense of mastery and competency and view difficulties as challenges rather than as failures.

The way adults criticise or provide feedback to children impacts on the development of pessimism and optimism. Children tend to criticise themselves using the same style of criticism that they receive from significant adults in their lives. When teachers blame failure on lack of ability they are teaching children to be pessimistic. 'John, obviously maths is not your bag. Writing is more your subject.' With this comment the teacher indicates that there is little the student can do to improve in maths because mathematical ability is presented as a permanent condition. If the teacher focuses on effort and performance rather than ability when discussing John's maths the seeds for optimism are sown. 'John, you obviously haven't put your heart and soul into the maths assignments recently. A more concentrated effort would probably bring the same results as you are getting in English.' The teacher focuses on factors that are temporary and changeable rather than on natural ability, which is permanent.

Similarly, criticism of children when they misbehave contributes to pessimism or optimism. When adults label the child rather than the behaviour they sow the seeds of pessimism because they point to failures in the child's personality, which is unchangeable. If you criticise a child as being a liar rather than someone who is not telling the truth, not only are they less likely to learn honesty, but you are focusing on permanence. When criticising or disciplining a child it is better to focus on behaviour (which implies specific and temporary causes) rather than blame the child's character or personality (which implies permanence).

The explanatory style of adults is a major contributor to the development of pessimism or optimism in children. Children are keen observers of the behaviour of parents and even teachers. When we criticise ourselves because we can't change a washer in the tap they notice; when we blame slow drivers when we are late they listen. When we blame our behaviours on our moods they take it in. When we blame bad luck for our inability to get a raise or even a job they are listening. Our explanatory style is there for children to absorb and internalise. Children not only hear our words but also see our body language; and even our emotional intensity is on display. Children have a habit of making their parents' explanatory styles their own.

Seligman found a high correlation between the explanatory styles of mothers and their children regardless of their gender. When a mother 'catastrophises' about negative events, blames herself and takes the view that there is nothing she can do to alter a situation, she is teaching her child to think the same way. Pessimists recycle their pessimism to their children.

The good news is that children are just as likely to copy their parents' optimistic explanatory styles as their pessimistic styles. When we congratulate ourselves for doing well, offer realistic responses about negative events rather than treat them as catastrophes of the highest order, and see hope rather than hopelessness when things go wrong, we present an optimistic style that children can adopt as their own. They need to see and hear optimism from parents and teachers if they are going to be optimistic themselves. That puts adults in powerful positions to assist the children in their care.

PROMOTING OPTIMISM IN KIDS
Modelling

So how can parents and teachers promote a sense of optimism in their children? Start by being aware of the explanatory style that you present to children. When things go wrong or negative events occur, do you view them as permanent or as temporary and able to be fixed? Do you take adverse events personally, blaming yourself for mistakes even if you are not directly at fault, or do you realistically apportion blame? Do you exaggerate negative events out of all proportion or do you take a rational view and realise that the sun will still rise even though the world may seem dark today? Okay, we all get down at times and life can look bleak due to adverse events. There are losses in everyone's life that involve a great deal of grieving before we can move on. Following times of loss we eventually need to present an optimistic face. The critical issue is the typical explanatory style that is on show everyday for your kids. Are you a gloom-spreader or possibility-pusher? Do yourself and your kids a favour and present an optimistic style so they can learn how to be optimistic themselves.

Teach the skills of optimism

Presenting a consistently optimistic explanatory style for children to observe and copy from a young age helps children develop optimism. Parents and teachers can take positive steps to teach children how to be optimistic and develop positive attitudes. But first you must learn the basics of optimism yourself. For preschool-age children the development of competency and masterful action are the tools for promoting optimism. These tools are covered in Chapter 6. Once a child is in school the attention turns to how they think – particularly when they fail.

Teach children to take realistic responsibility for events that happen in their lives. The key word is 'realistic'. Children need to learn equally that it is unacceptable to deflect responsibility for negative events and unhealthy to unrealistically accept blame for situations or events that are out of their control. Twelve-year-old Emily suddenly found herself ostracised from her peers at school. She was extremely hurt and was unsure how to react. With her mother's help she sifted through the events, not so much to seek a solution but to find where responsibility lay for the situation. Interestingly, Emily immediately drifted from one extreme view to another.

Initially she took no responsibility for the situation, preferring to blame her former best friend Kate for being the ring leader and 'making the other girls hate' her. Then she said that it was all her fault that nobody liked her. She thought that she was boring, a real square that nobody could possibly like. Both these views are unhealthy and are typical of a pessimistic explanatory style. Blaming herself indicated that the situation couldn't change because it was determined by her personality. Blaming others in some ways is healthier than self-blame because depressed people are forever blaming themselves when things go wrong. But blaming others is also an excuse for inaction. Emily's mother helped her daughter gain some perspective about the situation. She didn't let her off the hook and explained the place that her negative attitude played in breaking down friendships. On the other hand, her mother helped Emily realise that some aspects of her friend's behaviour contributed to the situation.

Teach a child to discuss behaviours rather than personality or resort to self-blame when things go wrong. Emily's mother was careful in her appraisal of the situation. She encouraged her daughter to consider the behaviour that might have contributed to her ostracism rather than her personality. This is important because optimists talk in terms of behaviour, which is changeable, rather than personality, which is out of one's control.

Encourage children to believe that positive events are determined not just by their behaviours but also by positive character traits. Optimists don't believe that positive events such as passing a test, playing a game well or getting a job happen due to luck. They believe that their efforts combined with personal qualities enable them to succeed. Optimists typically believe that 'I passed the test at school because I am smart' or 'I got the part in the play because I'm a good actor' and 'I got the job at McDonald's because I am good with people.' Qualities such as intelligence, talent or popularity are permanent and transferable to all situations, including negative events. Kids can draw on these qualities – their talent, intelligence or popularity – to help them when difficulties occur in the future or to repeat their success in other areas of their lives.

I am not suggesting that we should raise a generation of kids with egos the size of a football stadium or encourage young people to believe that talent alone will win the day. We should constantly remind young people that effort and hard work are essential ingredients for success or meeting challenges. But self-belief and a healthy ego can help. While humility is a welcome trait, we don't want to deflate a child's healthy self-belief in his or her abilities.

We already do a great deal in this country to dampen personal self-belief. Much has been written about the unhealthy attitude to achievement and success that exists. In the early 1980s the term 'tall poppy syndrome' was coined to describe our propensity to cut achievers and supposed high-fliers in corporate or public life down to size. As a nation we still have a tendency to take particular delight when anyone with an overblown ego fails or falls from grace. We do the same with kids. 'Big head' and 'show off' are just about the worst names you can call a primary school-aged kid. Parents who preach the virtues of humility over talent tell kids to pull their heads in, to stop showing off, and not to boast or boost themselves up.

I was reminded recently how parents teach kids not to advertise their talent too much when a friend paid a visit with his family. I began to chat with Donald, my friend's fourteen-year-old son, who told me that he had taken up art lessons. After describing some of his works he claimed, 'Actually I am good at painting – to be truthful I reckon I am very good.' I smiled at his confident self-assessment. Enter the dream-crusher in the form of his father who quickly cut his son down to size. 'Easy Donald', he said. 'Stop blowing your own trumpet. I am not sure a real artist would be as enthusiastic about your work.'

As I have already mentioned, we have developed a culture in schools where the belief that it is 'cool to be a fool' is dominant among adolescent boys. Consequently, they go to great lengths to hide their latent talents under layers of silly, even macho behaviours. And many girls have learned not to be too bright if they are to be accepted by their peers. It is okay to be attractive, good at sport and good at your schoolwork, but don't be *too* bright; if you are intelligent, don't rub anyone else's nose in it. These views predominate in many Australian schools at the moment. Thus the humility that we so fervently instil in our children has its price.

Optimism is all about attitudes which fuel belief, which in turn determines behaviour. If children see themselves as being capable and worthwhile then they are more likely to believe that they can positively affect events and experience success. The development of an 'I can' attitude is an essential part of optimism.

Teach kids to reframe negative or unpleasant experiences into positive events. While this may sound 'pollyannaish', looking for a bright side to experiences is a useful habit to teach young people.

Some examples of reframing negative events into positives are:

- 'You lost the Grand Final by a point but think how pleased you will be when you finally win.'
- 'You didn't do so well with that essay but you can pick up some valuable pointers for next time.'
- 'It is disappointing that it is raining and you can't go outside. But you can play some of those indoor games that you have been meaning to get around to for so long.'

Reframing is habit-forming. It can also be infuriating when something negative happens or you experience a disappointment and someone dismisses it by asking you to look on the bright side or find the silver lining. Recently I lost a day's writing when my computer broke down and I had forgotten to save my work. I was publicly lamenting my ill-fortune when my son reframed the situation for me saying, 'Come on Dad, you have a chance to do a better job with the second attempt.' The last thing I wanted at that moment was to be cheered up and reminded to look on the bright side, but he was right. I had no option but to do the work again and he made me focus on a positive aspect of the activity.

CHANGING YOUR CHILD'S AUTOMATIC PESSIMISM

If your child has developed a pessimistic view that affects the way they see themself, how they feel and how they interact with the world, you can do something about it. The following are some ideas to assist you to change your child's automatic pessimism. For further ideas I recommend that you read Martin Seligman's book *The Optimistic Child*.

Talk about self-talk

Most of us are not consciously aware of our self-talk but it is always there, giving us information, sending us messages, warning us against dangers and telling us what we can and cannot do, what we should and should not do. When I was young the nuns at my school referred to that inner voice as our conscience. They were extremely skilled at putting us in touch with our conscience – so much so that I recall on a number of occasions my inner voice screaming out to stop what I was doing because it was wrong, wrong, wrong.

Discuss self-talk with your child. Help the child to identify the voice in their head that gives directions, reassures them when difficulties arise and acts as a guide. Children who spend time alone usually recognise their internal voice immediately. It is important to reinforce that self-talk is perfectly normal – everybody does it. Help them to understand that their self-talk or thoughts influence their behaviour and the way they react to situations.

If your child can't identify their internal dialogue, ask them to look in the mirror and tell you what is running through their mind. Their internal voice will generally give a running commentary of what they see.

Teach your child the ABCs

Using a cognitive approach you can teach your child new ways to think and thus change their behaviour and reactions to negative or even positive events. You can help put your child in control of how they think and so influence how they feel and ultimately how they act. This approach can be used with children from approximately eight years of age. It was founded by Albert Ellis and Aaron Beck as a therapeutic tool, however it can be used by parents and teachers in a positive way to help children view events differently and to alter the way they behave.

This approach uses the acronym ABC. **A** stands for an adversity or an activating event such as a fight with a friend or missing a lift to school. The **C** stands for consequences of the event – specifically, how you feel and how you act immediately following it. The **B** stands for your belief about the event, which will determine 'C' or your response. The reason why one child will smile at and even embrace a strange dog while another will run away from the same animal is determined by their belief about dogs. One might have had nothing but fond experiences with dogs and has nothing to fear while the other child might have been bitten or scared by a strange dog so he believes that strange dogs are to be respected. The origin of the belief is irrelevant but it is the belief that determines the reaction when a strange dog enters the room.

To change 'C', the consequences or reaction to events 'A', it is necessary to change 'B', the beliefs about the events. Although this may seem complicated, we do it all the time with ourselves and with our kids. Have you ever told a child who is having a test at school that there is nothing to be afraid of, or that there is nothing to fear about a visit to the dentist. Perhaps, you have tried to persuade a nine-year-old that broccoli is really worth trying. Every child knows that a visit from Santa is a happy event. In each case it is the beliefs held about the event rather than the event itself that cause the emotions such as fear, loathing and excitement that determine their reaction. Imagine if Santa left no presents one year. What would be your child's reaction to Christmas the following year – unreserved enthusiasm? Hardly. The child would have developed a degree of scepticism about Christmas – their belief system would have been changed.

So use the ABC in a conscious, positive way with your children. When negative events happen, encourage them to look at the beliefs they hold. Use the following examples with your children to help them understand that their beliefs influence their feelings and behaviours.

If they were called over the loudspeaker to go to the principal's office, what would they think? They are in trouble? They will receive a reward for a good deed? They will receive some bad news? What is their self-talk telling them in each situation? What messages is their internal dialogue sending them? Their beliefs will affect how they feel and even how they approach the principal.

A friend called to cancel a trip to the movies that you had organised. How would you feel if they thought the following?

- The friend was sick and unable to attend.
- The friend was making up a story because she wanted to go to the movies with someone else.
- The friend was inconsiderate as usual, never thinking about anyone else.

Help your child identify emotional reactions to each possibility and their probable reactions according to each belief.

It's all in the brain

Much has been learned in recent decades about the operation of the brain in relation to learning. The chemicals (neurochemicals) that our brains release provide the basis for thought, memory, feeling and behaviour. Some chemicals rev our brains up when we need to do a task, while others are released to settle our brain activity down.

Long-term, consistent behaviour alters the baseline function of the brain. When we alter our thinking and our behaviour and create new habits, the neurochemistry changes as well so that new learning occurs. Our brain no longer reacts in old ways to negative and stressful events. New habits are accompanied by changes in brain chemistry that ensure the new habits continue.

One of the keys to raising positive kids is for them to understand that they are in control rather than at the mercy of events. It is not the negative event – loss, failure and/or defeat – that makes us feel helpless or hopeless; rather, it is our reaction to those events that leads to depression. The skills of optimism give children some control over the direction in which they head, even when they face difficulties and challenges in their lives. Optimism is one gift to place in your children's kitbag.

6

DEVELOPING A SENSE OF COMPETENCY

*Only when kids feel that they can safely
make mistakes will they begin to achieve their
full potential.*

UNKNOWN

Human babies are so dependent on their parents to satisfy most of their physical needs. In fact, the first two years of life are marked by the emergence from dependence or helplessness.

The move to independence is not necessarily a natural event. Dependence does not necessarily lead to independence. While young children do gain greater mastery over their world as they grow and develop, many parents unwittingly promote a sense of dependency rather than independence. They keep doing everyday tasks for children rather than allowing them and encouraging them to be active in resolving most of their physical and social problems themselves. The task of parents is, in a sense, to put themselves out of a job and promote a sense of independence through mastery and competence.

Recently I met a nine-year-old boy who could play a violin like a dream. It was quite remarkable how he could make those four strings sing. Yet his mother was concerned about him, claiming that he lacked a great deal of self-confidence. Even though he possessed terrific musical skills, he lacked basic social and personal competencies. This young boy who could play a violin like a virtuoso couldn't even make himself a basic sandwich. He was dependent on his mother to resolve most of his problems. She, of course, took up this task with relish, not allowing her son the opportunity to help himself. If he were hungry she would prepare his food. If he needed to go somewhere she would drive him. If he needed to ask another adult for help she would invariably ask on his behalf. She robbed her son of opportunities to develop the basic competencies of life and kept him in a state of dependence. It is little wonder he lacked confidence, because self-esteem comes from solving the ordinary tasks of living rather than from performing extraordinary feats.

COMPETENCY – THE BASIS OF SELF-ESTEEM

Self-esteem is a prerequisite for success in all areas of life. Most experts in the fields of education and child development agree that how children view themselves will determine their level of success in school and other areas such as sport, as well as the ability to form relationships. If children see themselves as competent and capable then they will begin to act in that way; in a way, a healthy self-esteem is a self-fulfilling prophecy. If children think they are capable based on their past experiences then in all likelihood they will succeed. On the other hand, if children view themselves as a failure then they will more than likely act in ways that produce those results and reinforce this negative view. The cycle of low self-esteem is an insidious one that is hard to break. Any failure that children experience merely reinforces the negative view that they have.

The origins of children's self concept are based on the feelings of worth that are formed in their early years. In fact, the sense of self-worth that children develop is largely determined by the age of two. Self-worth comes as a result of the bonds young children form in their early years. Parents promote children's self-worth through their loving contact, their human warmth and the respect with which they treat them. Young children build a sense of trust in their parents and believe that they are worthy of being loved, that they are lovable. Self-worth, the foundation for self-esteem, is not dependent on children's accomplishments but on their being. Self-worth is not boosted by any particular achievement but by the unconditional acceptance and love that they experience.

Self-worth can be changed and influenced as a child gets older, but the foundation is formed in a child's early, more vulnerable years – at infancy.

If self-worth comes from being, self-esteem comes from doing. A child's self-esteem comes as a result of their successes and accomplishments. It does not come easily; it does not magically appear after hearing a series of 'feel good' messages. When children interact successfully with the world they build their bank of accomplishments. When young children learn to wash themselves, even if they cannot perform the task perfectly, that is another experience to add to their repertoire, another experience to support a notion that they are capable, which is the basis of self-esteem. When a ten-year-old successfully negotiates their way to and from school using public transport for the first time, they make another addition to their bank of competencies; they find another reason to support their notion of positive self-esteem.

If self-esteem occurs as a result of children's actions then it is also situation-specific. A child's self-esteem may be high when they interact in some areas such as sport or in certain subjects, but lower in other areas where they don't feel so confident. When a child tries a new area of endeavour they risk failure. The extent to which children will extend themselves into new areas will depend to a large degree on their feelings of self-worth. The extent to which people love and accept themselves despite setbacks will determine their willingness to accept challenges and take risks. Self-esteem is like an onion, built from layer after layer of accomplishments, with self-worth at its centre.

The challenge for parents is to promote a sense of competency in children while teaching them about the appropriateness of behaviours and keeping them safe. It is difficult to do this without dampening a child's spirit or sense of determination. Two-year-old Thomas had a fascination with climbing over the couch in the living room. Janet, his mother, was intrigued by this behaviour but she was also exasperated by his continual attempts to hide in the space behind the couch. She tried distracting him but he was undeterred. She tried blocking the area off with a highchair but Thomas just climbed over that. She removed him to another room and closed the door. Thomas triumphantly pushed a chair against the door, climbed up on it and opened the door. He raced into the living room and climbed over the couch and lodged himself behind it. Janet peered over the couch and was greeted by a devilishly cute Thomas with a broad grin saying, 'Thomas did it. Thomas did it.'

Janet realised that Thomas enjoyed the challenge of climbing as well as testing his will against hers. She took him outside and provided some new climbing challenges for him to master. She realised that the obstacles she put in her son's way were just new challenges to overcome as he tested himself out and built up his repertoire of accomplishments. Rather than put her son down, she reminded him that climbing inside was inappropriate, and presented him with safe, more appropriate challenges. And she didn't take Thomas's persistence and determination personally. She was intent on channelling her son's persistence rather than trying to change him.

CREATING THE CYCLE OF COMPETENCY

The Harvard University Centre for Cognitive Studies found that for a child to move from a cycle of incompetency to a cycle of competency where learning and achievement promotes further learning and achievement a three-step process needs to occur.

Step 1: The stimulus of a model

A child needs to see a skill before they can learn it. Again, the impact of role modelling is important – in this case the most important factor in stimulating new learning and developing a sense of competency. Kids need to see parents perform a variety of skills. When children help or work alongside adults, whether it is helping to cook or load wood into a wheelbarrow, they witness first-hand the basic skills of living.

Step 2: Practice, repetition and variation

A child needs opportunities to practise and improve upon the behaviour that they have witnessed and learned. Patience is quite a virtue for parents – they must learn to step aside and allow their children to practise a variety of skills from feeding themselves to bed-making.

Step 3: Application

A child needs an opportunity to apply new skills to a variety of different situations. A child who learns to answer the phone invariably wants to do so every time the phone rings. Those same communication skills can be applied to other situations such as greeting visitors or giving presents to relatives at Christmas or birthdays.

Parents who join with children in performing the myriad tasks required of everyday life help create a cycle of competencey. When they provide opportunities for kids to practise a variety of skills that they have learned, either through observation or direct teaching, they are promoting the cycle of competency. When parents then provide children with opportunities to try out new skills in challenging or unusual situations they are completing the cycle of competency that is so vital for the development of self-esteem and further learning. This is a cheap, home-based activity that requires patience, time and faith in children's ability to learn and develop.

CREATING ENVIRONMENTS THAT PROMOTE A SENSE OF COMPETENCY

Some environments promote a feeling of competency and enable kids to develop a range of physical, social and problem-solving competencies. They encourage exploration and support learning. It is the psychological environment rather than the physical environment that is most important.

Can you recall your school days? My primary schooling had a mixture of environments. While the physical environments of most of my classrooms were similar, the atmospheres differed greatly. Some promoted a sense of personal competency and others stifled learning and took away any incentive to stretch myself and experience my personal strengths. I recall one class where the climate of fear of punishment for failure that the teacher created was so great that I, like many of my classmates, spent most of the year steering a safe path rather than step out of my comfort zone and risk failing.

It is adults who have the greatest influence over the environments that children spend their time in. Parents and teachers can create environments at home and at school that enable children to develop not only a range of abilities but a real sense of competency that comes from experiencing success, no matter how small.

1. Create opportunities and challenges

If we are to develop a sense of competency and mastery in children, adults need to provide them with opportunities to test themselves out and try new situations. Young children are at a developmental stage where they want to test themselves out and gain new competencies. They are also at a stage where they want to help out at home. I recall going to a regional city to give a parenting presentation. The organiser took me to the hall in the afternoon so I could check the venue and make any necessary changes. When I arrived, a three-year-old girl rushed to the car and tried to open the door for me. Seeing she was having trouble I opened the door, but she insisted that she hold the door open for me. She also insisted that she carry some of my papers so I walked at a snail's pace into the hall with my tiny helper by my side. It was a timely reminder that young children really want to feel useful and help those big adults who can dominate their lives and perform even the most menial tasks so easily. Sometimes we have to slow down and allow children to catch up.

It is through solving the ordinary tasks of living that children gain their sense of achievement. The promotion of self-sufficiency means that parents need to let go of some of their tasks. Do you take a toddler's cup from the table after a drink or do you ask the child to bring it to you? Do you make your children's beds or do you allow them to make their own? If your children can tell the time, do you allow them to take over the getting-up routine or do you still see it as your job to get them up each morning? Do you make children's breakfast or do they prepare their own cereal and toast? Do you cook each meal for your teenagers or do they cook for the family at least once a fortnight? If we wish to develop responsibility in kids we need to give them responsibilities. Similarly, if we wish to promote the skills of independence we must put kids in the position where they can learn the skills of self-sufficiency.

SUE, THREE-YEAR-OLDS AND DISHWASHERS

A friend, Sue, has positive expectations of her children. When each of her children was three she gave them the challenge of emptying the dishwasher each morning. At first she joined them, patiently showing which dishes to choose and where they were to be stacked. She soon allowed her children to unpack the dishwasher solo – plates included. Sue says they rarely dropped a plate and if they did she adopted an 'it doesn't matter' attitude.

When I tell this story during parenting seminars, many participants tell me that it sounds too good to be true. I remind parents that they only have to observe three-year-olds at play and they will invariably place a tray full of toys into some type of cupboard without any mishaps. Sue has her priorities in the right place. A few broken plates pale into insignificance compared with the message that she sends to her children by allowing them to perform this job.

It is relatively easy to promote basic competencies for young children, but it can be more difficult when they reach adolescence. They are less likely to want to help at home and want more time and freedom to pursue their own interests. Sometimes parents just give adolescents more of the same chores and jobs that they had when they were children. It is wiser to delegate some important tasks to teenagers and allow them to take responsibility rather than load them up with a whole stack of small jobs. Perhaps they can take charge of the garbage, the shopping or a significant area that challenges them rather than merely keeps them busy.

The hard part about enabling children of all ages to develop a sense of competency is that learning new skills takes time and requires patient adult interaction. When a four-year-old is learning to tie their shoelaces, they need time to fumble about and practise this difficult skill. They will become frustrated but that's okay. Adults need to stand back rather than rush or push the child to get it done – or worse, not give them a chance to do it. The practice of buying young children shoes with velcro instead of laces may be a godsend for time-strapped adults. However, a valuable learning opportunity is delayed.

Children also need opportunities to gain emotional mastery and to learn about relationships. They sometimes need their parents to help them work through their problems and emotions and relationship difficulties that they may have with friends or siblings. It is a concern in this busy era that many mothers and fathers lack the time to help children process and understand many of their new experiences. Parents can help teenagers in particular in this critical process by observing them and providing non-critical feedback when they feel it is appropriate.

2. Provide encouragement and support

Without encouragement and support, their [children's]
ability to learn, grow in intelligence, and bounce back
from adversity is curtailed.

E. TIMOTHY BURNS

Encouragement is the most powerful performance-enhancing skill that any human can learn. With real encouragement, a person can make a huge difference in the lives of those around them.

Parents often tell me that their child lacks social confidence or the confidence to try new activities. In most cases it is not a lack of confidence that prevents children extending themselves; rather, it is a lack of courage. Most learning involves taking risks. When we take risks in any endeavour then failure is a possible outcome, so children, like adults, avoid failure by not taking risks. Nothing ventured nothing gained.

Kids need plenty of encouragement if they are to gain a sense of competency. Encouraging people have the following attributes:

- They focus on the strengths of others rather than their weaknesses.
- They point out the improvement that others have made.
- They focus their comments on the effort, improvement or contribution that others have made.
- They have a positive attitude.
- Above all, they are persistent in their belief that others can achieve or do well.

Every adult who comes into contact with children has the ability to lift their performance through the powerful skill of encouragement. Unfortunately, most of us were raised by fault-finding methods where our mistakes and misbehaviours were pointed out so that our performance would improve. Right intent, wrong method. When we focus on children's deficiencies, they are likely to give up rather than try to improve, unless they are extraordinarily determined to succeed.

Did anyone that you know give up maths in school because they were tired of having their errors constantly pointed out?

If parents and teachers want to help children develop a strong sense of competency they should make encouragement part of their repertoire. The most powerful aspect about encouragement is that if children hear it enough they will give it to others. I had a first-hand lesson on the power of encouragement and its reciprocal nature when I achieved my surf-lifesaving bronze medallion. The eight-week course that I attended was a battle. Never a strong swimmer in my younger years, I found myself battling lack of fitness and advancing years as well as the waves. Part of the prerequisite was to complete a 400-metre swim through the surf combined with a run in less than eight minutes. It sounds easy, but it was not. Battling choppy 1-metre waves, the tide and cold wind, I nearly gave up on the second week of the program. As I came out of the surf, exhausted and well over the allotted time, there was my son standing on the beach urging me on. I cursed him but he just kept encouraging me to finish. Over the next six weeks I came close to quitting many times but my son just kept gently pushing me. He reminded me of my strengths as a person, he pointed out that I was improving my times each week and also reminded me of how good I would feel when I completed the task. He was so persistent with his encouragement that I couldn't dare give in. I completed the program and I am now the proud owner of a surf-lifesaving bronze medallion achieved in the chilly waters near the Southern Ocean, thanks largely to the constant, pestering encouragement of my son. I realised that all the encouragement that we had provided him when he experienced some early difficulties in school had sunk in and he was giving it back in spades.

3. Adopt a realistic attitude to mistakes

The third component of an environment that promotes competency and achievement is a realistic, healthy attitude to mistakes. Learning any new skill or behaviour requires a great deal of trial and error. Watch a baby learning to stand. They will fall straight away. They will get up again but usually will fall again. They will repeat this procedure until they get it right and their wobbly legs get the feel of standing. When we learn any new skill we go through a similar process to a baby learning to stand and walk. We generally don't get it right the first time but we will eventually succeed after many repetitions. A little bit of support helps as well.

In our rush to get things right, adults often don't allow children the luxury of making mistakes and learning from their errors. Besides, we were taught at school that errors were unacceptable. The schooling of a large proportion of the current generation of parents was based on the notion that mistakes were unacceptable. Smart students didn't make spelling errors and always got their sums correct. If they achieved nine out of ten for a test, the emphasis by parents and teachers was often placed on the one error rather than the nine correct answers. Thankfully, schools have moved away from this mistake-centred approach to one that encourages kids to explore different approaches and take risks in their learning.

4. Value effort and persistence

Adults and children should heed the message of the Chinese bamboo tree. The seed of the bamboo tree is planted and nothing happens in the first year. It still needs to be watered and fertilised. After two years there is no obvious growth but the tree still requires nourishment. After its third and fourth years there is still little growth. But some time in its fifth year it grows 30 metres. It didn't just grow in the fifth year but it took five years of watering, fertilising and nourishment. We can't always see the results of our effort straight away, but if we continue to put effort in, results will come. We just have to be a little patient at times.

Persistence is one of the greatest qualities that a child can possess. With persistence comes achievement and success. The child who keeps trying to learn, to acquire a skill or to improve in any area, despite setbacks, is one who is destined to experience success. Some kids give up easily when they experience frustration or lack of success. How many have tried music lessons but given up when it became too hard or changed sports when they experienced a lack of success? This is okay to a degree, but some kids continually change from activity to activity rather than work their way through difficulties.

Sometimes children's persistence is misplaced. Their determination to get what they want can be difficult for parents to put up with and is sometimes construed as misbehaviour. The toddler who continues to play in a forbidden area despite their parents' attempts to keep them out can be a trial. But the same determination to achieve a legitimate goal is one of the most useful attributes a person will have as an adult. Kids shouldn't have their own way if their minds are set upon something regardless of the consequences. Nevertheless, it is important to recognise that the blind determination that some children have to get their own way is actually a desirable attribute in many situations and one definitely worth preserving, even if it is the cause of considerable parental angst along the way.

5. Hold positive, high expectations

Expectations of children's behaviour and endeavours are usually self-fulfilling prophecies. One day a mother approached me after a parenting seminar and told me that her five-year-old son lacked confidence and was unwilling to accept responsibility. She claimed that she had to take care of most of his basic needs and she doubted if he could get by without her for even an hour. She also added that he was clumsy. She claimed that her son probably couldn't get himself a drink from the refrigerator. When I suggested that she let him try she said that he couldn't do it. 'He would probably just drop the container and make a mess.' Such is the power of expectations – if we think a child can't do something then they generally won't let us down.

Our expectations of children are conveyed through our behaviour and our language. Sometimes our expectations are obvious. Statements such as 'You can't do that' or 'You are a bit slow at maths' leave little doubt about our expectations of a child's ability to achieve. More often our expectations are conveyed in more subtle ways. We may unwittingly give more responsibility to one child than another, or quietly accept a child's mediocre efforts without question because we believe that they are not capable of any better.

Expectations can be tricky. If we have unrealistically high expectations for children's success and we continually point out their failure to measure up, then we run the risk of them giving up. Our expectations need to be grounded in reality and be achievable.

The key to positive expectations for children is to establish them when they are young. Help preschool and primary-age children understand that they have what it takes to achieve and succeed. Break complex tasks into simple achievable tasks so that they can experience feelings of success and raise their own expectations as well.

SOCIAL COMPETENCIES

Until now we have looked at how to help children achieve personal competencies that promote a sense of independence. These competencies or problem-solving skills help children resolve many of the problems that they encounter in their daily lives. Children also need to develop a set of social competencies that enable them to relate to and communicate with others and resolve difficulties that come from social living.

Children learn many social skills such as sharing and communication skills through their interaction with family members and their peers. Children need to be exposed to social skills if they are to acquire them. Parents, teachers and other adults and peers are suitable models for children to acquire social competencies, but kids need to be placed in situations where they can learn the skills of cooperation.

Five basic social competencies that all kids can learn are:

- sharing ... and caring for others
- being assertive – standing up for yourself
- asking for help
- resolving conflict ... and moving on
- making friends.

1. Sharing

Encourage children to share time, space and possessions from the earliest possible age. Sharing is an important element in forming friendships and is a prerequisite for living and working effectively with others. It is a vital skill for social and academic success at school. Parents can stimulate children to share by establishing a cooperative atmosphere at home. There are many situations in family life that can be used to foster cooperation and sharing.

SOME PRACTICAL WAYS TO PROMOTE SHARING:

- When serving sandwiches, place them on a large plate for everyone to share. Allow children to serve themselves from dishes at the meal table rather than putting food on plates for them.
- Use family discussions to teach children to take it in turns to speak and listen to others, which is an important social skill.
- Provide games and toys for the whole family to share. The rules of board and card games provide a good structure for children to follow.
- Limit children's time at solitary activities such as television and computers. Encourage interaction with other children through outdoor or indoor games.
- Promote a sense of generosity by encouraging children to swap or give away old toys.
- Share television time with other members of the family.
- Provide an opportunity for a child who has difficulty sharing to occasionally play with younger children or even toddlers. It is often hard to avoid sharing with younger children.

Talk with children about sharing. Let them know that it is okay not to share sometimes, particularly their treasured possessions. Find out their concerns and discuss solutions. For instance, explain to a child who is reluctant to share that they should show the borrower how to take care of a toy.

...and caring for others

As social beings we are happiest when we contribute to our own well-being and the well-being of other people. When children are young, helping is generally confined to home, with perhaps the occasional opportunity to help a neighbour or relative. Teenagers should be encouraged to contribute in some way to the broader community. The notion of community service is unfashionable at the moment but its benefits for kids and the community are enormous. Community service enables young people to experience the power of helping others and belonging through useful ways. Community service takes many forms, including assisting and teaching younger children, coaching a sports team, assisting older people and taking part in a group community project.

In parts of the United States where community service by young people is actively promoted the outcomes have been extremely positive. Not only do kids form connections to their local communities through worthwhile involvement, but also the community perception of young people invariably becomes more positive.

2. Being assertive – standing up for yourself

Assertiveness is a skill that young people can learn. An assertive response helps them to stick up for their rights and avoid being teased or bullied. Assertiveness involves the use of a firm voice and strong body language, including body positioning and eye contact. Assertiveness indicates control and implies an expectation of compliance. Aggression, on the other hand, shows lack of control and involves a raised voice, the use of insults and body language that often inflame a situation, inviting further aggression or provocation.

SOME IDEAS TO HELP YOUR CHILD DEVELOP
ASSERTIVENESS:

When a child or young person is being provoked, bullied or teased they should do the following:

- Make eye contact, standing in a balanced, comfortable position about a metre from the person who is doing the provoking.

- Using a firm voice, ask the other person to stop what they are doing. Use their name if possible.
- Repeat the response if they don't stop.
- If the provocation continues they should walk away, ignore them or seek an adult if they feel that they are in danger.

When a child or young person needs to stand up for their rights, ask for something, make a statement or be listened to rather than ignored, they should:

- Gain the person's full attention.
- Be polite and use the person's name.
- Make good eye contact and use a strong stance.
- State the request or statement using a firm voice.
- Give the other person an opportunity to respond if appropriate. Ask questions to clarify the other person's position. Be polite but firm and avoid personal insults or using a whining voice.

Encourage your child to practise assertiveness in low-risk situations – in front of the family or even in front of a mirror.

3. Asking for help

Kids need to understand that it is okay to seek the help and assistance of others when they experience difficulties of any type. Asking for help is part of being human, not a sign of weakness. Unfortunately, many adults are not adept at seeking assistance from others when they are in trouble. This is symptomatic of our present social climate of individualism where stoicism is seen as a virtue. We have an extensive vocabulary devoted to stoicism. 'Grin and bear it', 'Ride it through', 'She'll be right', and so forth.

To hell with stoicism! At times we all need some help from others, whether it is a shoulder to cry on, someone to off-load our troubles to at the end of a hard day or someone to ask for a loan to tide us over when things become tight. I can't help but wonder whether our present epidemic of male suicide is caused in some small way by the cult of stoicism and would be relieved if males could just learn to ask for help. Kids need to see both males and females talking about their problems in an atmosphere of general support and empathy. But first they must see their parents and other significant adults ask for help.

4. Resolving conflict ... and moving on

Conflict is part of social living. Conflict exists between family members and also occurs between friends regardless of age. Children, teenagers and adults have disagreements that need to be resolved. Dealing with arguments and disagreements protects relationships and allows feelings to be honoured.

Young children's disagreements can be noisy and sometimes physical. They often lack the skills to resolve conflict in socially acceptable ways. They will usually learn these over time if they have witnessed healthy conflict resolution within their immediate environment. Some children need help to resolve conflicts that they have with others.

SOME IDEAS TO HELP KIDS OF ALL AGES RESOLVE CONFLICTS

Two basic rules of conflict resolution to observe are:

- Avoid calling others names, shaming or looking to blame others.
- Hitting or physical means are out.

Teach kids to:

- Stay calm when they become involved in a dispute. If they can't stay calm they should move away and return when they have their anger under control.
- State their point of view and how they feel about the situation that sparked a dispute. 'I felt rotten when you played with the others and left me by myself.'
- Listen to the other point of view without interrupting.
- Search for a solution that suits both people. If they can't find one then they should move away, but not let the disagreement spoil their friendship.

5. Making friends

Friendships are important for happiness and well-being, particularly around adolescence. This is a stage when kids can be cruel, sometimes excluding others from peer groups for little apparent reason. Girls often form close and intense friendships as they enter their teens. They often have best friends, which change dramatically from one day to the next. Boys tend to form looser and less exclusive social groups often based around mutual interests. It can be lonely for a child or young person who is isolated from peer groups or without a best friend.

SOME IDEAS FOR HELPING KIDS MAKE FRIENDS

- If possible, establish a dialogue with your child about friendships so that you can support them when they have difficulties and give them some ideas when needed.
- Identify and discuss any behaviours such as teasing, bullying or self-centredness that may prevent your child from making friends. Sometimes a child's remarks can irritate others to the extent that they become ostracised.
- Teach some social skills such as how to start up a conversation and how to hold the interest of others during a conversation.
- Provide opportunities for kids to have friends at your place after school or on weekends so that friendships can develop. An invitation to bring a friend along to family outings and holidays can provide opportunities to strengthen friendships.
- Encourage your child to participate in out-of-school activities or groups that may provide opportunities to meet new people away from the peer groups at school. Friendships formed through shared interests are often very strong.

- Encourage your child to take up a challenging or interesting activity so that he or she becomes a more interesting person for others to be around.
- Image is usually important for adolescents, so you may need to make some compromise about issues such as clothing and appearance in order that acceptance by peers is maintained.

TEACHING KIDS MANNERS

Teachers at my children's primary school placed good manners on the curriculum. No, they didn't teach children how to hold a knife and fork correctly or how to call for a waiter in a restaurant without drawing undue attention to themselves. They began with the basic social protocols of saying 'please' when they want assistance and 'thank you' when they receive it.

Although this is not exactly progressive education practice, they should have been applauded for teaching kids just about the most effective social skills that they will ever need. There is little doubt that the way we ask for something affects the outcomes. We can gain cooperation from anybody, including less-than-compliant kids, if we just ask in the right way. Basically, that means using good manners.

The best way to help children to gain social skills is through the age-old standards of teaching and modelling. Kids need to see adults use common courtesy when they interact with each other and with them. Personally, I sometimes find that difficult, particularly when I am busy and I just want to get things done.

One time I found myself hurling orders around at home trying to coerce my kids to help me fold some washing. Receiving little interest, I changed tack and quietly approached them, saying, 'Could you please help me fold and put away the washing? It would be a great help.' No sarcasm, no grovelling, just a basic well-mannered request for help. It worked. I had the assistance I wanted in a flash.

Sometimes parents look for all types of strategies to gain cooperation when a little basic courtesy is all that is needed to do the trick.

Of course adults need to remind kids constantly to use manners. It can be monotonous but it is worth it. Sleepovers, outings, school camps and other occasions when parents are not around are the true test of kids' manners. As a teacher, I used to find that if social protocols were taught at home then they would generally be on show in adult company when the children's parents were not around. It is frustrating how kids always seem to save their best behaviour for anyone but their own flesh and blood.

One way to get the message across is to refuse to cooperate with children until they use manners. In one family I know, a request that is not accompanied by a please draws no response from parents. The mother reasons that such a method is better than constantly reminding kids. It saves wear and tear on her voice box, she claims.

I saw a bus driver use this principle when a fifteen-year-old passenger yelled out, 'Hey driver! Turn up the radio will you?' The driver promptly turned the radio off. The fifteen-year-old, who had a great deal of front but obviously not a huge vocabulary yelled out, 'Hey!'

The driver stopped the bus, quietly turned to him and said, 'Sport, try using some manners and see how you go. I generally only do things for people who show me a bit of respect.'

He was my kind of guy. He showed that he was no doormat and expected respectful treatment. The adults on the bus who heard this encounter all nodded their heads in approval and the fifteen-year-old tyro sheepishly left the bus mumbling something about 'I'll show you bloody manners'. I had the distinct impression that it wasn't his stop but he had lost face so a quick exit was in order. The walk would do him good and give him time to think!

A friend had a novel way of making sure her four-year-old remembered his p's and q's when he spent a day with his grandparents. She gave her son a paper bag just before he left the car and said, 'Sweetheart, this bag is full of pleases and thank yous. Enough to last the whole day. I want to see the bag empty when I pick you up.' Sometimes you have to make things very concrete for young kids.

Mealtimes offer a great opportunity to teach kids some social graces. More than teaching basic manners, a shared meal accompanied by some chat provides kids with the opportunity to hold a conversation, which many adults find difficult. It is the simple social skills learned at home that count the most.

So next time you catch yourself reminding your kids to say please and thank you and to use other common courtesies, tell yourself that you are doing them a favour. More than merely teaching them to show respect for their elders, you will be providing them with a very effective means of getting cooperation from others. It is amazing how far they will go in life if they develop the habit of using some common courtesy.

7

HELPING CHILDREN DEVELOP EMOTIONAL LITERACY – MATTERS OF THE HEART AND SPIRIT

Parents have to be smarter about how they teach their children basic emotional and social lessons.

DANIEL GOLEMAN

At a recent business meeting I saw a man break down in tears as he answered a question that was posed by his superior. The question was a mundane one about an aspect of work that didn't warrant such an emotional response. He apologised profusely and later admitted surprise about his reactions. He explained that the question triggered memories about a recent trip to the battlefields of Gallipoli, which affected him deeply. His tears took him by surprise – 'How long has that been lurking there?' he said later. All through his trip around Gallipoli he didn't shed a tear and then four weeks after his return the tears flowed, triggered by a harmless question. 'What is it with emotions that they can lurk there and sneak up when you least expect them?' he said.

As a society we are more knowledgeable than ever about matters of mind and body, but less sure about matters of the heart. We know how to look after our bodies. Eat healthy food, exercise regularly, cut out the smokes, cut down on alcohol consumption and not only will you increase your chances of living longer but your well-being will improve as well. Most people are well versed in this type of message and more people than ever heed the healthy living credo.

There has also been greater awareness about how to improve our minds and the quality of our thinking. Expand your mind with the right input – less junk television, more reading – and not only will you dazzle guests at dinner parties but you will have greater job prospects and more chance of success in all areas of life. The right thinking will put you on the road to success; think positive thoughts – lots and lots of them – and success will generally come. Sportspeople and businesspeople alike now celebrate the power of visualisation as they use their imaginations to help them on the road to success. Whole industries have sprung up helping us keep our minds and bodies in good order, but now it is time to turn our attention towards our emotional well-being.

The revolution has started. After decades in which the logical and the rational in human relationships have been promoted, there are now moves to consider the importance of the inner world – that lesser known part of the human psyche that is a person's emotions.

Parents, educators and other professionals have become proficient at providing for the minds and bodies of children. We can teach them all sorts of skills and knowledge that will help them get jobs; we can teach them social skills that are transferable to many situations. We have become proficient in developing children's minds and bodies but we have not been so competent about helping children understand and handle their troubling feelings. Emotions are often seen as problematic rather than welcomed. In schools, kids are often discouraged from showing excessive positive feelings. Excessive excitement, happiness and joy can be difficult for teachers to contain. Expressions of anger or sadness are often fobbed off with a 'she'll be right' attitude or statements such as 'Come on, get over it. It'll be right in the morning.' This is not meant as a criticism of teachers or parents. Teachers have not been trained to deal with kids' emotions. As class sizes increase it is harder for teachers to give kids the attention they need when they are feeling troubled. And most parents have been conditioned by their own parenting experiences to attend to their children's language, behaviours and attitudes – the overt stuff they can see and hear. The emotional world lurks somewhat deeper and is less obvious. We tend to see the behaviour triggered by feelings and we deal with that; it is easy to see and attend to a child's hitting-out but the possible anger or frustration behind the behaviour is harder to fathom and not so obvious.

The results of failing to learn about emotions are becoming increasingly obvious. With depression and suicide on the increase among our young people as well as increases in other problematic behaviours such as eating disorders, it is important that we help young people attend to their emotional world in positive ways. The terms 'emotional literacy' and 'emotional intelligence' are now gaining currency. Researchers such as Daniel Goleman, John Gottman and others are now pointing to the benefits of raising children who are emotionally literate or emotionally intelligent. These terms refer to the recognition of a person's emotions and the ability to find outlets for them in positive ways. After a decade of research, Gottman found that children who were raised to be emotionally literate were better at regulating their own emotional states, related better to others, and were more likely to develop empathetic qualities. With such qualities it is little wonder that they succeed in social areas, being more likely to make and keep friends than other children. Significantly, those children who had developed strong emotional intelligence had parents who attended to their emotions and helped them deal positively with their feelings.

PROMOTING EMOTIONAL LITERACY

Research has found that parents tend to fall into two broad categories concerning the way they handle children's emotions: those that provide their children with guidance and assistance and those that dismiss or disapprove of their children's emotions and offer little support or assistance. Those that assist their children neither object to – or ignore – their children's displays of anger, fear or sadness. Instead, they recognise their children's emotions and help them find solutions to their underlying problems. These parents also help children find acceptable ways of expressing their emotions and place limits on unacceptable behaviour such as hitting others when they are angry.

Parents can start with the way they tend to a distressed child. When they respond to cues of distress, fear, overstimulation or excitement and attempt to calm the child down by rubbing their back, turning them over and/or giving them a blanket to stroke, they are promoting their child' emotional intelligence and promoting self-soothing behaviours. When parents soothe their young child they are teaching them that they can move from one state to another and that the negative emotion has a purpose, which can satisfy a need. Kids who remain overstimulated may not get the chance to calm themselves by sucking their thumb or rubbing the soft silky part of a blanket.

Emotional literacy is a key tool for life that parents and educators can promote in children from a young age. Helping kids deal with their emotions is not necessarily a step-by-step process or a neat set of pointers to follow. However, parents can help their kids deal with their feelings in the following ways:

- develop an awareness of their own emotions
- practise empathy
- develop a vocabulary for emotions
- use emotional moments as opportunities to solve problems
- set limits for behaviour.

1. Develop your own emotional awareness

Are you cued into your own emotional life? Are you aware when you feel angry, sad, happy or jealous? Does it take a blowout before your feelings become apparent or do you tune in early when you are distressed? In truth, most people go about their daily lives blissfully unaware of exactly how they are feeling until the first hunger pangs hit. Many of us avoid situations that may lead to conflict, anger or pain, or we cover up our feelings. Worse still, some of us do our best not to feel anything so we distract ourselves by eating, watching television or by some other diversion to take our minds off our negative feelings. Much of this is unintentional.

Most of us operate on a rational or cognitive level. Our conversations are sprinkled with the vocabulary of reason: 'I think that ...', 'I can't believe ...', 'What do you think about ... ?', 'If only we could think of a better way to ...' This is the way we have been conditioned by our own parents and by education systems for years. A friend of mine always challenges me because she communicates on an emotional level. Her conversation invariably forces me to explore how I feel about issues, situations or people. A telephone conversation is littered with comments such as 'How are you feeling today?', 'You sound frustrated about ...', 'How do you feel about that situation?', 'How would you feel if we tried to ...' She is adept at communicating on an emotional level even over the phone and can reflect back to me how I may be feeling without using visual cues, which is quite a skill.

Both males and females can develop a deeper awareness of their emotional lives. Meditation, prayer, artistic expression and diary-writing are common ways to tap into your feelings. Gottman, in his book *The Heart of Parenting,* advises parents to record or log their feelings over a period, noting what incidents might have triggered different emotions and to record how they reacted. Gottman maintains that our feelings become more manageable and less frightening when they are written down. Being aware of your own emotional world will help you to be more sensitive to your children's feelings (that is not to say that their feelings will be easy to understand). Kids often express their feelings indirectly in ways that adults can find confusing.

2. Practise empathy

Walk a mile in another Indian's moccasins before you make a

judgement.

NATIVE AMERICAN SAYING

Parenting is always a dilemma and nowhere is it harder than when we confront children's feelings. How many of us have brushed aside children's fears, nerves or other negative feelings either for the sake of expediency or in the belief that if kids can suppress or push away their negative feelings they will be okay? I recall brushing off one of my children who, as a five-year-old, was nervous about a trip to the dentist with an 'It'll be okay' type of attitude. It would have been better to at least acknowledge her trepidation and talk about how she might cope.

Listen with your eyes as well as your ears

Empathetic listeners use their eyes and their ears to tune into children's emotions. Facial expressions, body language and gestures all provide clues to how a child may be feeling. A furrowed brow, slumped shoulders, tense jaw or that relentlessly tapping foot are all signs that kids may be upset or feeling troubled. There are no hard and fast rules about reading the emotional signs of others, so intuition or gut feelings are important guides. It helps if you know your child well and are tuned to what's normal behaviour and what's not.

I remember driving my three children home from school a few years ago and being surprised by my son Sam's aggressive behaviour towards his two younger sisters. His jaw jutted out and his language was spiteful; both were out of character. To be truthful, it didn't take an Einstein to work out that something was bothering him. My immediate reaction was to reprimand him about his anti-social behaviour, but something told me that a strong rebuke wouldn't be well received so I quietly reminded him about appropriate behaviour and gave him some time to be by himself. At this stage I had no idea what might have happened at school or what was going on in his world – except that he was upset about something.

After half an hour or so I thought it was time to talk with Sam. I chose his bedroom, knowing he would be more relaxed and likely to open up in the safety and familiarity of his own turf. I approached him by asking if I could sit down for a bit. 'You seem upset', I ventured.

'No I'm not.'

I continued. 'The way you spoke to your sisters was not you. You seem annoyed with something.'

'I am.' Then as if the floodgates opened he told me about the difficult time that some of his supposed schoolmates were giving him.

It seemed that he was on the receiving end of some serious teasing and he was not sure how to deal with it.

This was not the time to give him advice or help him explore some options. It was simply the time to listen. Sometimes the hardest thing for a parent to do is to listen to their children when they are experiencing difficulty and resist the temptation to offer advice. At this point all that was necessary was for me to listen to my son and let him know that I understood how he felt. One lesson I have learned in life is that there is nothing better than to be understood by someone else.

It takes time

It takes time to be attentive to kids and their feelings. When we are busy or rushed off our feet we are less likely to be aware that something may not be right in our children's worlds. We need to give them our undivided attention when we listen to their stories. Melissa told me how her eight-year-old daughter came home from school upset because she was left off the invitation list to her best friend's birthday. Melissa had an appointment in half an hour but she thought that she would help her daughter deal with her hurt. They both sat down but Melissa was obviously rushed. As her daughter opened up about how hurt she felt, Melissa had one eye on the clock knowing she had an appointment to keep. She couldn't relax. Her daughter picked up on her mother's tension and she became annoyed with her mother's lack of attentiveness. This was obviously not the time for empathetic listening. Melissa admitted she should have given her daughter a cuddle and given her an opportunity to talk later that evening when she was in a more attentive frame of mind.

3. Develop a vocabulary for emotions

Help kids find the words to describe how they are feeling. Gottmans's research indicates that the simple act of giving emotions a name can help children contain and recover from their troubled feelings. Somehow when we give a feeling a name it doesn't seem so unknown or scary; it helps bring it to the surface.

Suggest to children how they might be feeling but be careful not to tell them how they should feel. Sometimes labelling kids' feelings is a matter of trial and error, as in this dialogue between a concerned parent and their child:

'You seem really angry about being left off the team after you trained so hard.'

'No, I'm not mad at all.'

'I guess it can be disappointing not to get what you want when you work so hard.'

'Yeah it is rotten.'

The more precisely kids can name their feelings, the more helpful it will be. If a child is angry, he or she might feel mad, bitter, disappointed, left out, frustrated or hurt. The vocabulary that you use will depend on a child's age and their ability to comprehend.

4. Use emotional moments as opportunities to solve problems

Do you see a child's emotional outburst as a crisis or as an opportunity to help resolve an issue and develop intimacy? If you are just about to serve up dinner to your hungry family when one child belts another in anger, this is not necessarily the time to practise your empathetic skills and conduct a meaningful conversation to reach your child's inner world. There is a time and a place for everything.

But children's negative and challenging emotions can provide you with the opportunity to help them soothe themselves, resolve a problem or be close to a parent. Often it is when children are upset or hurt that we have the opportunity to talk and comfort them. Many men tell me that helping their children when they are upset, angry or scared makes them feel like fathers.

Children's negative feelings usually dissipate when they talk about them, label their feelings and know that someone understands them.

Helping a child find a solution to a problem can be tricky. Children under the age of ten have difficulty holding more than one option at a time, so brainstorming is generally out when helping young children. It is usually suitable to provide a suggestion or two and allow them to try the ideas out. Generally, the best solutions are those that children think of themselves, so avoid taking over the problem-solving. I recall a conversation with my young daughter that went something like this:

Sarah: I hate it when Kate won't let me play with anyone else. She just wants to play with me.

Me: That would be pretty annoying not being able to play with your other friends.

Sarah: It is. I hate it.

Me: What can you do about it?

Sarah: I don't know. I like playing with Kate on the weekend but during school she is a pain. I've tried hiding but that doesn't work – she always finds me.

Me: That's one idea. Have you tried playing chasey or some other game that needs lots of people?

Sarah: No, but no-one really plays those games at school right now.

Me: Any chance of just suggesting a game to your friends? You seem to have no trouble at home getting others involved.

Sarah: Yeah, I could do that.

So the conversation continued as I helped Sarah generate a solution for her dilemma. She certainly needed some prompting as she seemed bereft of ideas. The important part is to engage children in finding their own solutions while maintaining a balance between exploring options and giving them ideas.

Helping adolescents find solutions is easier. They are generally capable of brainstorming and evaluating a number of possible solutions, however you may need to remind them of the efficacy of some solutions. I can recall assisting teenagers to find solutions to their social problems and patiently pointing out that revengeful actions such as hitting or embarrassing others may be natural reactions but are not generally in their long-term best interests.

One successful problem-solving technique is to draw comparisons between a current problem and past successful solutions. If, for example, your child is upset at some unfair treatment by a peer then encourage them to look back and pinpoint strategies that have been successful in the past. Help evaluate the usefulness of each idea;

ignoring a friend's teasing might have been suitable in one situation but may not be suitable in another.

5. Set limits for behaviour

It is important for children to understand that all feelings are acceptable but not all behaviours are. It is okay to be angry but it is not permissible to hit a sibling, break a toy or call someone names due to anger or frustration. Children need to learn that their feelings are not the problem but their actions are.

There are no hard and fast rules about the behaviours to limit, but parents need to take into account the age and stage of the child, the particular circumstances and their own values. Psychologist Haim Ginot introduced a useful set of guidelines for parents. He encourages parents to think about children's behaviour according to three zones: a green zone, a yellow zone and a red zone. The green zone includes desirable behaviours that we encourage freely in children and the red zone includes behaviours that cannot be tolerated regardless of the circumstances – those that are unsafe, illegal, unethical or immoral. These two zones are easy to discern and leave little to adult discretion. Ginot's third zone, however, is challenging to parents as it requires them to use their discretion and common sense when dealing with children. The yellow zone includes behaviours that adults don't condone but may tolerate for either of two specific reasons. The first is 'leeway for learners'. A four-year-old may have difficulty sitting at the table for more than five minutes at a time, but you expect they will get better with maturity. So you may turn a blind eye to inappropriate behaviour even though some other four-year-olds can quite easily sit for ten minutes without a problem. The second is 'leeway for hard times'. A teenager may challenge a mother's authority at a time of divorce or a child who is being bullied may act in a hostile manner to his or her siblings. While you may not approve of such behaviour and let your child know this, you may tolerate it or turn a blind eye when it occurs. This is not necessarily excusing poor behaviour but there are times when we need to take into account extenuating circumstances and use our common sense as a guide when dealing with children.

Time alone

A mother in a parenting group indicated that she was concerned that her twelve-year-old daughter spent too much time alone in her room. She wasn't sullen or moody but suddenly she was spending more time alone – usually lying on her bed staring at the wall, doodling or constructing jigsaw puzzles. In my opinion this girl needs to be congratulated for finding a great way to draw on her own inner resources. In effect, she was dealing with the stresses of life (she had just begun secondary school and was undergoing major bodily changes) through contemplation and reflection. It is a tremendous asset to look within and find your own way to soothe and relax yourself.

Address low-level feelings before they escalate

I was watching my fourteen-year-old son fixing the wheels on his skateboard. He was having trouble removing the ball bearings, which had seized, and I could see that he was working up a full head of steam. Noticing his agitation, I said quietly, 'That looks like hard work. A bloke could burst a boiler trying to get those ball bearings out.' He looked up and smiled at me. What was becoming a full head of steam began to dissipate before my eyes as he took some deep breaths and began to relax.

Sometimes we wait until children have thrown a full-blown wobbly before we turn our attention to their behaviour. There are times when a humorous comment or observation can be all that's needed to prevent a highly-charged emotional outburst – its all in the timing!

Emotions that manipulate

Have you ever seen a child throw a tantrum? Of course you have. Most of us at some stage use tantrums to get our own way. Young children generally choose the noisy throw-themselves-to-the-ground variety when they don't get their own way, while adolescents often choose door-slamming or abuse of their parents to regain control of a situation. Having outgrown these noisy tantrums, adults opt for more subtle types of persuasion such as the nose-in-the-air sulk, which is far more socially acceptable. Tantrums, regardless of the form they take, are a type of emotional blackmail. They also require an audience for them to continue – the bigger the audience the better. So supermarkets, shopping centres and friends' homes are common places for children to strut their stuff. Even teenagers who throw tantrums in bedrooms do them loudly enough for their parents to hear.

Recognise the intent behind tantrums. They are an effective method of regaining control of a situation or of getting what you want. It is pointless trying to remonstrate with a child in the middle of a noisy tantrum. It is better to be firm and refuse to be blackmailed. Remove yourself (if this is safe) or quietly remove a child from the scene. When the heat of a tantrum subsides, discuss with your child better ways of getting what they want or expressing their feelings.

Encourage kids to verbalise the bad stuff

A family I know discourage their children from having harsh or unfriendly words with each other. This is not healthy. It is better to encourage children to verbalise their differences – even letting each other know how they may feel. To put it bluntly, kids are less likely to thump each other when they have the opportunity to verbalise their feelings. Of course, they should do so without derogatory statements about physical appearance, gender or other personal put-downs.

KIDS WITH CHARACTER –
THE DEVELOPMENT OF POSITIVE
VALUES AND QUALITIES IN KIDS

*What lies before us and what lies beyond us are tiny
compared to what lies within us.*

HENRY DAVID THOREAU

What is it that sets some people aside from others and helps them achieve and succeed? What is it that helps some people rise above difficult and adverse conditions and leaves others floundering about, never quite making it in life? Natural ability to perform at whatever their chosen field is a contributing factor. There are many sportspeople, artists and budding entrepreneurs around but only a handful ever rise to the top in their field. Good fortune plays a part. You may get some lucky breaks but even with all the luck in the world people can squander their talents. The difference between those who are successful or lead fulfilling lives and those who squander their talents can be attributed to qualities and values that contribute to a person's character.

One of the basic tenets of this book is that while people are free to choose how to think and act, they are strongly influenced by the environments in which they interact from an early age when their self concept is being formed. Free will is one thing, but our thinking is influenced by those we mix with and the messages we receive.

Part of the job of teachers and parents is to pass on a set of values to their children. Values are at the base of every culture. They determine how we relate to each other, how we behave and also how we act in the world. Values are the framework upon which we base our behaviour. They act as inner guides to provide direction for the way we conduct much of our lives.

Children are exposed to many messages from a variety of sources about who they are and how they should behave. For example, television advertisements for sportswear often show athletes performing amazing feats accompanied by messages aimed at inspiring people to succeed and achieve. These are fine sentiments but rather simplistic. Parents and teachers need to give some semblance of balance to these types of messages. Kids are being exposed all the time to messages about how to act, think and even what to wear from sources that don't necessarily have their best interests at heart, so parents as social agents need to be aware of the values and qualities that they promote in their children.

This is not to suggest that we control children or try to engineer outcomes, but we need to be aware that children are developing a sense of self that comes with a value system and set of personal qualities so we may as well model and reinforce those qualities and values that will help them lead successful, purposeful lives and be positive tools for living.

CONGRUENCY

The way parents raise children is a reflection of their own values. If you wish to raise children to respect others then you need to use child-rearing methods that are respectful of your children's basic human dignity. Smacking and other hurtful methods are incongruent with this value. Similarly, parents who want to promote initiative and independence in children have to stand back and allow children the space and opportunity to develop these qualities. One well-meaning, loving mother I know claims that independence is her guiding principle, yet she is a virtual slave to her children, doing everything for them. Presumably she will wave a magic wand when they are eighteen or so and they will magically become responsible, independent beings capable of standing on their own two feet and looking after themselves.

A father I know sent his children mixed messages – his behaviour didn't support his rhetoric. For years he urged his children to be tolerant of other people and to respect and celebrate our differences. He diligently reprimanded his children for any slurs or personal insults they might have uttered based on race, gender, sexual preference or personal appearance, but he was put to the test when a gay couple moved in next door to his home. At first he said nothing, but over a period of time his intolerance of their different lifestyle came to the surface as he continually made disparaging remarks about everything they did, from the way they kept their garden to the contents of the rubbish that they left out. He discovered that there were limits to his tolerance and this was obvious to his children, who let him know that his treatment of his neighbours was based more on their preference of sexual partners than any other rationale. If your values are to give children direction, they need to be in congruence with all aspects of your life.

SEVEN POSITIVE VALUES THAT EMPOWER CHILDREN

There are seven values that empower kids to form successful relationships and achieve personal success and that guide them through the difficulties that they will encounter. These are respect, persistence, initiative, self-discipline, trustworthiness, tolerance and cooperation.

Respect

Respect is the central value around which all successful human interactions revolve. Respect means treating others with dignity and recognising their rights to be treated safely and fairly. If a person is to be respectful to others then he or she has the right to be treated with respect too. Respect, then, is reciprocal.

I often hear that children don't respect their elders as they did in the previous generations. This is true to a point. One obvious example is the way children address adults. When I was young, children always called adults by their surnames and uncles and aunts usually had those titles attached to their first names. Today kids tend to use first names when addressing adults. The notion of respect has shifted away from being hierarchical (respect your elders and your superiors) to being more mutual (respect each other regardless of age, sex or race). This is a small but important shift that means children have a right to respectful treatment just as adults do.

Respect is evident in all our interactions with others. I recall a colleague many years ago bending down to talk to my preschool-aged children so that she could make eye contact with them. She also used to greet them with the same enthusiasm that she greeted adults, showing that they had equal status in her eyes. These were small tokens of respect that are often not given to children. Parents show little respect for children when they interrupt them in mid conversation to speak to another adult or walk into the bedroom of a teenager without asking permission.

Respect means not giving in to others for the sake of peace or expediency. Parents need to remember that they have rights too so they don't always have to give in to others. Sticking up for yourself is a sign of self-respect.

Parents can promote the value of respect by:
- using the term when interacting with children: 'When you treat me rudely you are not showing me any respect.'
- modelling the value by maintaining your child's dignity particularly during discipline. Methods such as embarrassing your child, smacking, shaming and criticising them show little respect for their dignity.
- respecting yourself. The notion of self-respect means that you expect respectful treatment from your children. Although at times they may be less than perfect in their treatment of you, don't be a doormat.
- teaching children to use manners when interacting with others. Manners are social conventions that ensure the respectful treatment of others.

Persistence

Have you ever seen a child really want something so badly that they will not be dissuaded regardless of how often they are distracted, how many rebukes they receive or how many obstacles are put in their way? We curse such kids sometimes and parents rue their misfortune for having such an obstinate child. But when kids apply that same type of persistence to achieving a positive result in school or sport we are the first to honour their ability to stick to a task. We reframe their obstinance as single-mindedness or strength of will. Stubbornness is reframed as persistence.

Persistence or determination is a quality in children that adults celebrate in some instances but actively discourage at other times. I just love watching my daughter play basketball. She is so determined to succeed that she chases down every ball and runs the length of the court to defend, even if there is only a slight hope of retrieving the ball. I cheer her persistence. But that same determination is also displayed at home at times when she fights hard to stick up for her rights or merely to delay her bedtime by five minutes. At these times I curse her determination and give it another name – stubbornness – and I wish momentarily that I could change it. But her determination and sheer persistence needs to be encouraged, not changed. It is a wonderful quality, although as a parent it is my job to help her channel her persistence into positive pursuits without dampening her tremendous spirit. Through trial and error she will learn when determination is an asset and when it is appropriate to gently give way for the sake of expediency.

Initiative

I heard a radio interview recently where the interviewee, an executive with a large multinational corporation, was bemoaning the fact that his company couldn't find people who used their initiative in the workplace. According to the interviewee, most employees could follow instructions but had difficulty initiating action or taking a lead when needed.

There is little doubt that those young people who are prepared to make things happen rather than sit back and wait – or, worse, bemoan their bad luck – are those who will get the good jobs, make the team or get their desired results. This is not about positive or wishful thinking but about common sense. The world waits for no one; it moves on with or without you. Initiative is not about being pushy, rude or obnoxious but about people taking responsibility for their circumstances and making things happen.

Problems and difficulties surround children and our reaction as parents makes a huge difference. We can create opportunities for them to resolve their problems or we can solve them ourselves. When a child claims to be hungry we can invite them to use some initiative to resolve the problem or we can prepare the snack ourselves. If you choose the former course be prepared for some creative solutions and messy kitchens, but that is part of the learning process.

In my family, anyone who takes an irresponsible position and waits for something to happen or complains about a situation is invited to use their initiative to resolve the situation. Recently, one of my children sat shivering in front of a wood-fuelled heater whose fire had long gone out, complaining that she was cold. Basically, she was inviting someone else to fix her problem. She was promptly reminded to use her initiative, rather than wait for someone to fix her problem. She relit the fire herself using far too much firewood but that was okay. If we are to encourage children to make things happen then they will make mistakes. One way to extinguish a child's initiative is to criticise them when they make an error.

A DISPLAY OF INITIATIVE

An eleven-year-old boy who was an exceedingly resourceful individual was serving me in a woodyard. I asked for a small amount of wood (about 250 kilograms) which was all that my small trailer could carry. The weighbridge was out of order so he couldn't weigh my car to work out its load. I said that I would go elsewhere, but this young boy was not about to let a customer get away. His father, the owner of the woodyard, was attending to another customer so the young boy resolved the problem in his own way.

He directed me to back my car up to a small set of scales. He filled up a handbarrow with wood, weighed it on the scales and then filled my trailer by hand. He repeated the process until I had the required amount. I couldn't help but admire his resourcefulness and his work ethic, so naturally I gave him a hand.

I complimented the boy's father when I paid my bill. He told me that his son showed tremendous initiative at work, however at school his work ethic and resourcefulness were not evident. His father said that the requirements of school did not suit his son, who felt more comfortable in the hands-on environment of the woodyard. Sometimes it is not the child who is the problem – it is a matter of finding the environment that enables the child to prosper and belong.

Self-discipline

Self-discipline or internal control is one of the most important abilities for a child to develop. Self-discipline refers to the ability to moderate or control behaviour to achieve desirable outcomes. Anything worthwhile in life takes effort to achieve and generally requires you to give something up, subjugate your immediate pleasure or put up with a little disruption or discomfort. If you want to improve your fitness then it may mean getting up earlier each morning, giving up certain foods and changing some entrenched habits. It requires discipline or self-control to stick to your fitness plan despite the distractions and inconvenience to your lifestyle that it may cause.

It is unfashionable to talk about self-discipline in terms of child development. However, it is part of raising children. Children who are able to practise impulse control and delay self-gratification have a huge head start on others in all areas of their lives. A child must exercise self-discipline many times each day and sometimes it is easier than others. For instance, most children find that getting to class on time without being reminded by a teacher is relatively easy. Years of conditioning make it an automatic response for most students to stop what they are doing and head off to class when the school bell sounds. It takes more self-discipline to turn off the television at home and head to a bedroom to complete homework. That is a tough one for many students, but it is necessary at times if they are to experience the rewards of study. The trouble is, the rewards for study often aren't as obvious as the instant gratification that comes from watching television.

It is hard to promote a sense of self-control in children if parents assume all the responsibility for their behaviour. Most of us take on far too much responsibility for our children's behaviour – we do so because we want to protect them from harm or hurt. If children experience real danger then parents need to act swiftly and take control of a situation. However, there are times when parents need to sit back and allow their child to experience the consequences of his or her decision. If we want self-discipline, children must be able to make decisions and then change their behaviour accordingly.

As children become older, talk to them about the need for self-discipline and control. They need to understand that to achieve anything worthwhile they will have to give something up and apply new habits. That is the way of life.

Trustworthiness

Trustworthiness means that a person can be relied upon to keep his or her word. It means others can rely on them regardless of the situation. Trustworthiness is a vital trait in both the worlds of work and relationships. Without a sense of trust, agreements mean very little. Trustworthiness is a tremendous self-esteem builder. When others trust you to keep your word or to rely on you to complete a task no matter how tough the distractions are, then the message is that you are a worthwhile person. A person can send no greater message of faith than to let someone else know that they trust them.

'My parents don't trust me' is a common lament among teenagers. My answer to adolescents with this refrain is that to be trusted by others it is necessary to act in ways that engender trust. Gaining someone's trust occurs by being reliable and honest in small dealings. Coming home at an agreed time, completing homework rather than watching television and doing jobs without reminders are ways that adolescents can engender their parents' trust.

Trusting an adolescent is one of the biggest tests for parents. In fact, there comes a time when parents can do nothing else but trust their children to do as they say they will. This means that parents must be careful not to expect too much or have unreasonable expectations of their children. Some parents put their adolescent children in such impossible positions that they have little option but to betray their trust.

Teach children to be trusted without making them feel ashamed

To develop a sense of trustworthiness in children it is best to start trusting kids when they are young and practise in relatively safe situations. That way you have established a habit by the time the important stuff happens later on and you have little control over your young person. I remember when my son, who was then ten years old, was required to complete his homework before he was able to join some friends for a game. Once his work was finished he raced out of his room to join his friends. He suddenly stopped and asked me if I wanted to check his work to make sure that he had done it. I thanked him but refused his invitation, as I trusted him to do the work that he had agreed upon. Trust means not checking.

There are times when children will betray our trust by not sticking to their bargains or even telling lies to keep up appearances. Rather than moralising about telling the truth or shaming them by letting them know that they have let us down, it is more effective to talk about the implications of betraying someone's trust. To be trusted is a privilege and affords a person greater freedom than not being trusted. Kids need to learn that if they are not trusted then they will not be given the same freedom to decide as someone who is trusted – that means they have to be home earlier, have homework checked regularly and the like. It is the consequences of their decisions rather than moralising lectures that teach kids about behaviour.

Tolerance

Young children are naturally very tolerant of the differences of others. In fact, young children are blissfully ignorant of the physical, social or intellectual differences of other people. They accept people on face value, making decisions based upon intuition or experience rather than skin colour or other superficial things.

Tolerance is an empowering value as it forces a person to be not merely accepting of others but flexible. A person who practises tolerance is less likely to blame others for mistakes or try to change them. Tolerance requires a person to change and be more patient, forgiving or accepting. Tolerance doesn't mean allowing others to hurt you but it does mean accepting and appreciating differences, whether they be in point of view, way of life or appearance.

Parents can promote the value of tolerance by:

- encouraging children to focus on improving themselves rather than trying to improve others
- modelling a tolerant attitude when they talk about others
- being patient with others
- discussing topical issues with children and respecting their views
- challenging children's points of view if they are not based on fundamental rights of fair treatment.

Cooperation

Cooperation is often confused with compliance or obedience. The latter refers to falling in line with or abiding by the wishes of others. Cooperation refers to the ability to work together with others for the welfare of all.

Cooperation cannot be bought. In a family sense, many parents try to buy their children's cooperation by paying them to help around the house, offering bribes if they complete homework, or even rewarding children for eating with offers of sweets if the vegetables are consumed. This is not promoting cooperation but rewarding compliance and obedience.

Influence rather than persuasion obtains cooperation. It is based on the notion that we work together for the good of all. Before we have cooperation we need mutual respect to exist.

The folly of competition

Competition and cooperation cannot exist side by side in a family or classroom. By definition, competition means defeating another person by getting a higher score or winning the race. It means winners and losers. Cooperation, on the other hand, implies that no-one wins unless everyone wins. I have known parents to claim that they promote cooperation in their families yet they actively encourage their children to compete with each other in sport and in schoolwork by comparing children's results. Not only is this a dubious way of encouraging better results but it promotes sibling rivalry based on competition.

Competition may be great on the sports field and in the workplace but it has no place in relationships or in families.

One plus one equals three

When individuals combine to work on a project their efforts multiply. Two people working together will generally produce better results than two people working side by side but separately. The ability to cooperate and work together is rapidly becoming a desirable workplace skill.

A FINAL WORD ON VALUES

It is strange how adolescents, in a bid to stand on their own two feet, will reject many of the ideals that their parents hold most dear. I remember coming home from school as a sixteen-year-old and announcing that I was to become a communist. I wasn't sure of the implications of such a move but I do remember that I enjoyed watching the discomfort that this caused my parents. Such a move was flying in the face of their beliefs and values. But the enduring values that my parents lived, breathed and acted out every day of their lives have stayed with me – or, rather, I have returned to them. Values such as giving others a fair go, treating everyone with respect, being honest in the way you deal with others, valuing a strong work ethic and many others that direct my life still remain. They are part of my parents' enduring legacy that helps shape my character.

Part 3

IT TAKES A WHOLE VILLAGE TO RAISE A CHILD

A young mother in a parenting presentation asked for some ideas to keep her two-year-old twins busy when she put her three-year-old daughter in her car seat. They had a habit of running away at such times, particularly when she was in a shopping centre. Picturing a mother struggling to supervise young children while pushing a shopping trolley through a suburban carpark, I remarked how hard it must be raising three children so young. She quickly informed me that she had four children under four, not three. It was obvious that this mother wanted help, not just a few management strategies. She was playing a lone hand in the most complex job of all – raising children.

Raising kids needs to be seen as a community responsibility. The most effective parents are those who have heaps of help from a variety of sources. In our increasingly mobile society, many mothers and fathers are separated from their extended family and the wisdom and practical help that they can offer. Children also benefit from exposure to large networks of adults who have their best interests at heart. Grandparents, relatives, neighbours and family friends all play a part at different stages of kids' lives. Members of the broader community such as sports coaches and guide leaders are also important members of a child's community network

Parenting is rarely done well in isolation. The demands of raising children are too much for one or two people. In fact, there are times in kids' lives when parents must step back as another adult such as a teacher, a boss, a coach or a relative has a greater direct influence than they do. The socialisation process means that other people must take over from the parents at some stage, supplementing the work that they do. Even children raised on vast cattle stations in remote areas of Australia are linked to broader communities through radio education and other technological means.

The world that parents present is too narrowly focused and too homogeneous for children's healthy development. For adolescents, the views and beliefs of their parents can be stifling so they need to mix with responsible adults who have different opinions from their parents and an array of lifestyles that open up possibilities for who they may become. Family, local community networks and institutions such as schools provide a diverse array of people who can add colour and richness to a child's life as she or he grows into adulthood. Part 3 looks at how schools and the broader community can contribute in positive ways to the lives of children and young people.

9

WHAT SCHOOLS CAN DO

*Kids can walk around trouble if they have some place
to walk to and someone to walk with.*

MCLAUGHLIN

There will always be a place for schools in the lives of kids. In the future, schools may not look exactly as they do today but they must still be there. Schools are great socialisation agents, providing opportunities for young people to grow to adulthood in safe environments and in structured ways. At the moment, Australian schools are much more than places of learning. Most are social welfare agencies as well. For many children, their teacher is the most stable person in their lives – at the very least they are always there. For many parents, too, their child's teacher or a senior teacher at their child's school are the only reliable allies they have when facing family or personal difficulties. Those people are the first port of call for an increasing number of parents experiencing family trauma or distress.

For those who work in them, schools are demanding places right now. High student–teacher ratios, expanding curriculums, complex kids, kids with complex problems and the demand for teaching styles that account for individual differences can make schools hard places to work in. But – and here's the rub – teachers and the schools that they inhabit have a massive influence on kids' thinking, behaviour and attitudes (even if it is negative), so we need to do everything in our power as a community to ease the load and provide schools with the resources and all the morale-boosting support that can be mustered. There is little doubt that at the centre of every vibrant, healthy community that supports kids there is a school or school system that is vibrant, healthy and supportive of kids and staff.

TEACHERS ARE LEADERS, NOT JUST MANAGERS

The significance of teachers in the lives of children is often underrated. American educator Pat Munson in her 1991 paper 'Winning Teachers/Teaching Winners' stated:

> *The front of the classroom is a powerful place to be. The responsibility is awesome. You cannot teach and empower children to be successful if you do not hold yourself to be so. Everything you are and all that you believe is transmitted to your students at some level. We owe it to our students and ourselves to be sure that who we are and what we believe is really our truth.*

The core person in a school from a child's viewpoint is a teacher. If a child is in primary school it will be *the* teacher; in secondary school a number of teachers are involved. Although the relationships may not be as intense for secondary school students, teachers are nevertheless important. At the start of the year, primary school children will base most of their judgements about the coming year on their teachers. Sometimes this assessment is way off the mark; the teacher who has a reputation as the meanest in the school often turns out to be a softie or 'the best teacher I've ever had' for many kids. Teachers are in a position to inspire children and young people or turn them off learning, to make them feel good about themselves or feel inadequate. Not every teacher will reach every child or make a difference. For some kids, the teacher will not make any difference at all, no matter how dedicated they are or how stimulating the program is that they organise, or how caring they are. But the law of averages states that if you are in front of enough kids for enough time enough of them are going to be touched by you in certain ways.

POSITIVE ROLE MODELS

Teachers, who spend a significant time interacting with kids, are significant role models. If ninety to ninety-five per cent of all learning occurs from modelling and for five hours a day teachers are the only adults that kids are exposed to, then their behaviour, attitudes and thinking are just as critical as the subjects they teach.

The influence of modelling is pervasive. Not long ago I observed a Year 5 class at the request of a school principal. She was concerned that many of the children in the class had attitude problems and as a result were not only highly critical of each other, but also often just plain nasty in the way they treated each other. After observing the class in action for an hour I understood exactly why the principal was concerned. The children in the class were very quick to criticise and put each other down for the slightest mistake. Their teacher did the same. Even when giving her students positive feedback she always added a qualifier or a personal put-down. 'You got those maths problems correct Jason. Well done. But they could have been presented more neatly.' Many of the children in the class used the same language and even the same gestures and facial expressions as their teacher when they criticised each other. It is human nature to adopt the predominant attitudes and behaviours of the environment you are in. As leaders, teachers need to set the tone for a class rather than react to it, and be positive models for children. If we are to have positive kids then we need positive teachers as role models to show them the way.

TEACHERS AS OPTIMISTS

I pray that my children will always be taught by teachers who have an optimistic view of the world. Optimists make great teachers because they have so much faith in children's ability to succeed. Their optimism shows through their positive expectations for success and is often reflected in the challenging or exciting programs that they establish for kids. Optimists are generally enthusiastic about learning and motivate their students through their passionate involvement.

Pessimistic teachers cripple kids with their attitudes. Their lack of belief in kids, which is really a lack of self-belief, holds students back and prevents them from taking risks and extending themselves. Pessimism shows in the language they use: 'Don't be silly, Soula. You won't be able to run that fast in a month of Sundays', 'Troy, your sister was a real star in school. What's your story?', 'Come on lift your game. You don't want to be stuck at the bottom of the pack forever do you?'

It is not just a child's learning that is affected by a teacher's pessimism but their thinking too – particularly when they fail. When a teacher focuses on poor results, exaggerates negative events out of all proportion and focuses on a child's personality when things go wrong, he or she displays a pessimistic explanatory style for children to absorb and internalise. I am not suggesting that teachers be constantly positive or always put on a bright, cheery face. Life's not like that. Teachers get tired and put up with a lot of disturbing behaviour. Like everyone, they feel down at times and negative, which is reflected through their language; that is human nature. Kids know when a teacher is tired, stressed or in a bad mood. Smart kids are adept at reading their teachers' moods. (Teachers need to be supported so that they don't fell stressed and out of control, but that is another issue.) It is the day in, day out explanatory style that some teachers adopt that can be so harmful for children. A year in a class with a pessimist for a teacher can be a long haul for any child.

Optimistic teachers:

- teach children to take realistic responsibility for events that happen. Children need to learn that it is unacceptable to deflect responsibility for events that involve them, but that it is unhealthy to accept blame unrealistically for situations or events that are out of their control: 'It's all my fault that the relay team lost.'

- refer to behaviours rather than personality when kids misbehave or have difficulty with their learning. This is important because optimists talk in terms of behaviour, which is changeable, rather than personality, which is out of one's control.

- encourage children to believe that positive events are determined not just by their behaviours but also by their positive character traits. When a child performs well in a maths test or plays a good game of netball it is not due to luck or good fortune. Talent, intelligence or qualities such as persistence that are permanent and transferable to all situations play a part in success. Kids can draw on these qualities – their talent, intelligence or persistence – to help them when difficulties occur in the future or to repeat their success in other areas.
- reframe negative or unpleasant experiences into positive events. Putting a favourable gloss on events is a powerful motivator for children and can present them with possibilities that they didn't think about.

PRINCIPLES OF POSITIVE SCHOOLS

The protective factors that form the basis of resiliency are powerful principles that can exist in families and communities and within schools. Schools that truly value relationships, hold high and positive expectations for children, staff and parents and create opportunities for meaningful participation lay a foundation for kids to learn the skills to live healthy, fulfilling lives.

Nurturing relationships

Teaching is first and foremost about relationships. Physical resources, buildings and curriculum are all important but they are peripheral to what is really vital about schools. The primary relationship that exists in schools is between teacher and student. The secondary relationships are peer relationships, which are in part fostered by teachers. Kids expect many things from teachers, with fair treatment, plenty of encouragement and an interesting curriculum being of primary importance. But longitudinal studies from Australia and elsewhere leave no doubt that students primarily want a teacher who cares about them and has their best interests at heart. That may sound a little simplistic, but what separates the good teachers from the memorable is not teaching methodology or subject knowledge but intangibles such as passion for the job and an ability and real desire to form relationships with students.

It is fascinating to talk with people about their school days. Usually they begin by reminiscing about old friends and the good times that they shared. Then most people will generally recall a special teacher who really left a deep impression on them. They remember the teachers who took that extra special interest in them, who went beyond the subject they taught. They made a real attempt to connect with kids as the people. Some people I have spoken with have experienced 'turnaround teachers' – those teachers who had such an impact on them that they helped put their young lives back on track after seemingly going off the rails. Significantly, E. Timothy Burns writes about a study of drop-outs from US schools where few if any of the respondents could 'recall any teacher who they could consider a friend throughout their school years'. Above all else, in education it is the caring ethic of teachers that makes the huge difference to kids.

Caring in school is not some mushy, abstract concept that is practised by a select few in schools such as the student welfare coordinator or practised when a person is in trouble. There are many definitions of caring, but I prefer Bonnie Benard's version. She says, 'Caring in school is seeing the possibilities in each child and using one's wisdom of the heart [when teaching them].' The effect of the caring ethic is best illustrated in the following account of a school bus driver provided by an American school administrator (in Bonnie Benard *Fostering Resiliency in Urban Schools*).

I recently visited a rather progressive school district in Arkansas. As I was working in one of the schools, one of the teachers told me that her students were quite distressed because their bus driver was retiring. She had repeatedly tried to get her students to accept the driver's retirement, but she felt that she had failed. She asked me if I would talk to the children. I agreed and asked her to tell me all she knew about the bus driver.

'I know his name is Mike', she told me, 'and that he appears to be quite kind. However, he usually has trouble getting his bus loaded on time after school.'

My talk with the children was brief. All they could do was express their distress at losing Mike and they asked me to make him stay 'cause he's our friend.'

With only one thing left to do, I went looking for Mike, who turned out to be a very pleasant-looking man in his mid-sixties. I apologised for intruding into his business and assured him that I was not trying to dissuade him from retirement. 'I am only interested in learning why the children, in your opinion, hold you in such high regard,' I told him directly.

Mike said that about three years earlier he had overheard the principal tell the teachers that a corporate purpose had been adopted and described this purpose as the need to get the kids to believe in themselves and be proud of their accomplishments. Mike had been on the route for a long time and knew that most of the kids went home to an empty house. He also told me he noticed that the kids often left school papers on the bus, even the ones with stars and smiley faces. He concluded they had no-one to share the papers with when they arrived home. Keeping the new purpose in mind, Mike began asking the students as they entered the bus to show him the papers that made them feel good.

'Do you think I did the right thing?' he asked me. 'It does take longer to load the bus.'

While the caring ethic of teachers is vital, the role of caring peers and friends in the healthy development of children cannot be overlooked. The ethos of the school can either promote or hinder the level of support that children provide for each other. A school-wide ethic of care is demonstrated in the level of staff collegiality, a curriculum that values cooperative learning techniques and classrooms that take the time and effort to promote peer relationships and cohesiveness through group games, shared experiences and shared goals. The caring ethic is more than just a strategy or a program; it is a way of people conducting themselves so they convey compassion, respect and interest in others.

High and positive expectations

A wise teacher once said that the best thing you can do for students is never feel sorry for them. She reasoned that when we sympathise with a child due to difficult circumstances or because of some physical or intellectual disability we immediately lower our expectations of that person. And holding low expectations is just about the most harmful thing you can do to a child.

There is little doubt that those schools who hold positive and high expectations for each student not only have greater rates of academic success but reduce the likelihood of emotional and behavioural disturbance as well. This, of course, is placed in a context of a caring atmosphere and balanced programs that cater for a wide variety of interests. High and positive expectations for students are demonstrated through an emphasis on achievement, clearly stated rules and boundaries, high student participation and a variety of academic and extra-curricular activities.

The self-fulfilling nature of expectations is so powerful that students tend to live up to or down to them. Researchers have demonstrated that students who were previously labelled as 'slow learners' were able to excel when placed in accelerated learning programs. Successful teachers look beyond the exterior, see the gem that is inside and communicate this vision back to the child. When the messages that children hear from both home and school are that they are capable then they will naturally form this image of themselves.

Effective teachers know that the curriculum needs to cater for the interests and abilities of their students. This concept has been the foundation of good teaching in most western countries since the 1970s. The danger inherent in this concept is that in an effort to cater for a student's interest and teach at their level, teachers run the risk of lowering their expectations or at least failing to suitably challenge students. An example of this strategy has been the proliferation of child-based interest literature that not only uses themes that kids can easily relate to but utilises their language as well. This is done in an effort to encourage more children to read literature. This strategy makes terrific sense, however, in an effort to encourage more children to read, educators run the very real danger of not lifting students' sights high enough or providing them with material that really challenges them. Effective educators look for children's interests and strengths and use them as starting points to extend and challenge students to achieve.

Schools communicate their expectations of students in the way that they structure and organise learning. Positive expectations of students' ability to learn and extend themselves are shown when:

- there is a varied curriculum that gives all students the ability to be successful
- teachers organise programs that cater to a broad range of learning styles and multiple intelligences
- a multicultural curriculum exists that values students' home cultures
- student motivation comes from involvement and experiences of success rather than a reliance on external motivation that comes from reward and punishment systems
- discipline is based on fairness and respect, and promotes a sense of responsibility in students.

Opportunities for meaningful participation and contribution

Australian schools are more interesting places than they were a generation ago. New subjects, hands-on learning and engaging resources are just some of the attractions of modern schools. But by far the most significant shift in terms of teaching methodology is the move by many schools to involve students in more meaningful ways in their education process. The move to active involvement is not a program change but a shift in school culture, which is shown through participatory teaching methods within the classroom and a willingness to share power outside the classroom. Fundamentally, it requires a shift in teachers from being an instructor to being a facilitator of learning or to shift from being the 'sage on the stage' to being a 'guide on the side'.

Active, meaningful participation is shown when the strategies of shared decision-making, cooperative learning, peer help and mentoring and multi-age classrooms are used.

Shared decision-making

The willingness by many schools to involve students in decision-making at a school and classroom level is significant. This provides kids with the opportunity to influence and act on their environment rather than merely being at the mercy of others. People need to participate in the decisions that will affect their lives; this is closely linked to the need to have some level of control over one's life. The notion of control is at the heart of promoting positive, proactive kids capable of taking their place in the world of the twenty-first century. Schools that operate under democratic principles involve kids in decisions that affect what they learn and how they learn and also about how classrooms will operate. This doesn't necessarily mean that teachers give up power, rather that they share it with their students. Student representative councils, classroom meetings and group discussions are the tools of democratic schools and classrooms.

Cooperative learning

Cooperative learning is a powerful strategy that challenges students to work together collaboratively. It can occur in all subject areas and is not restricted by age. In cooperative learning activities, students draw on each other's strengths and work towards a common goal. Cooperative learning strategies promote social competence and help students develop problem-solving skills such as the ability to plan and utilise human resources. It is little wonder that the skills of sharing and working together are highly regarded by most employer groups.

Peer helping and mentoring

Peer helping and mentoring has been used in some form in schools for decades. In my school days, teachers would often ask a student who finished early to help a child who was struggling or needed extra assistance. I remember on the occasions when I was asked to help a classmate feeling very special indeed. Obviously my self-esteem received a boost, but I remember the special feeling that comes from helping someone to acquire a skill or concept that you already possess. Sometimes when you learn something new all you want to do is teach it to someone else.

Helping someone else is a self-affirming activity. Many schools now formally incorporate mentoring and student helping activities into their programs. In primary schools it is common for senior students to visit the classrooms of younger students to engage in joint learning ventures. Schools that use formal mentoring or buddy systems report a decrease in bullying behaviour and improvements in social behaviours and academic results for the mentors. It is the older kids rather than younger ones who seem to benefit most.

Multi-age classrooms

The move towards the establishment of multi-age classrooms that is gradually occurring in Australian schools needs to be applauded. The traditional way of grouping of children in same age classrooms assumes that the teacher is an instructor and the sole focus of learning. However, children learn a great deal from each other. They need to be seen as resources rather than products and provided with opportunities to be teachers as well as learners. Multi-age classrooms provide kids with the opportunity to be both teacher and learner as they work together rather than just alongside each other. Such classrooms enable them to learn problem-solving skills and develop social competencies and the skills of autonomy and independence in a real-life, family-like structure.

10

HEALTHY COMMUNITIES FOR KIDS AND PARENTS

---

*We are, inherently, village people. The trick is to
recognise that the dream of village life is a dream
about how to live, not where to live.*

HUGH MACKAY

It is a paradox that the larger a community becomes, the more we
tend to shift responsibility to others for problems both big and small.
From my experience, the more a school population increases, the less
personal it becomes and the more it relies on systems and
organisational strategies to get things done. It is no coincidence that
large schools often have difficulty getting parents along to help at
working bees and in canteens, whereas small schools usually have
more success at getting the parental help they need. Rather than leave
it to someone else, parents are more likely to roll up their sleeves and
help out.

In western countries in the twentieth century there has been the
strange phenomenon of urban dwellers retreating behind front fences
to be safely cocooned in their own homes. Urbanised living means
that community problems and issues always occur in someone else's
backyard. It is not that people aren't community minded. The
generosity that Australians routinely show following natural disasters

such as bushfires and floods shows that community spirit is alive – it just takes a significant event for it to come to the surface.

Raising kids, which was once seen as at least a broad family concern is now the sole responsibility of parents, albeit supported by schools and other agencies. The term 'parenting', which has gained currency in the 1980s and 1990s, is indicative of where we place the responsibility for raising children – squarely on the shoulders of mothers and fathers. Undeniably, parents play the major role, but raising kids needs to become part of community consciousness rather than purely an individual responsibility.

Once churches were the cornerstones of communal life. In the past, people were attached to a church at birth through the ritual of baptism and tended to wear their religion like a badge. Religion might have added very little to a person's spiritual life but it generally gave them a sense of identity and attachment. Churches have traditionally been anchors for people during hard times. Whether they lost a loved one or needed a handout, people in the past turned to their church community for support. With most churches reporting waning congregations, not only are we losing the important social glue that holds many communities together, but parents have lost a strong ally in the birth-to-adulthood process of raising children.

SURROUND KIDS WITH POSITIVE PEOPLE

Raising kids is too important a job to be given to parents alone. Kids should be surrounded by caring adults from birth to adolescence – adults such as teachers or coaches who come in and out of their lives and other adults such as family friends or relatives who are always there. The breadth and variety of experiences that other adults can provide adds a hidden dimension to a child's life that parents alone cannot give. Kids who are brought up with limited access to adults are the poorer for it.

Parents are often quick to judge or admonish their children, whereas other adults who are not weighed down by parental hopes and dreams are more accepting and sometimes more fun to be around. There have been times when I have been overly critical about my own children's behaviour, dress, schoolwork or some other mundane aspect of their behaviour. Then a friend visits and brings me back to earth by giving them a friendly smile, an accepting joke or just showing genuine concern. It is always easier to remember what it was like to be young when you are with other people's kids. It seems that the children of other parents are always better behaved and easier to manage, get better marks in school and will probably have better futures than our own children. If only we could bring up other people's kids! Children benefit from the broader perspective that adults who aren't burdened with parental responsibility can offer.

ISOLATION

It is easy for parents to feel isolated from their community. With the increased participation of mothers in the paid work force and with people working harder than ever, the opportunities to be actively involved in community life have diminished. Family life and work can be all-consuming so we have little time or energy left to create or maintain social networks. But parents need to become active, at least socially, in the community for their own well-being and the sake of their children. It takes time and effort for people to establish links within their community, but it is worth it for their own sakes and the sake of their children.

WHEN PARENTS JUST WON'T DO

There comes a time in the lives of many adolescents when they look outside their immediate family for someone to take on the fathering or mothering role. For many girls and most boys, at the age of sixteen or seventeen their same-sex parent becomes off-limits or an object of fun or derision. The parent who was so adored by a young child can be practically despised by an adolescent. The parent held up by a child as the paragon of wisdom suddenly knows nothing – and, what's more, they never did according to some teenagers. Australian author Bryce Courtenay described this phenomenon in his book *April Fool's Day*:

I discovered with all my sons that one morning they wake up and their world has changed. Instead of being happy kids they are morose and silent. Instead of quite liking their parents they now see them as practically mentally retarded … Everything 'sucks' … their voices drop an octave and they temporarily lose their ability to speak, this facility being replaced by a Neanderthal grunt which covers every possible situation they confront.

Desperately trying to keep a distance between themselves and their parents, many adolescents benefit from a relationship with someone outside their immediate family. Sports coaches, neighbours, uncles, aunts, even older brothers and sisters can fill this important role in kids' lives. When kids are breaking away from their parents they need someone apart from their peers to take an interest in them, keep an eye on them and talk to them. My brother, who is six years my senior, filled this role for me. I remember as a sixteen-year-old being given such a lecture after a bout of drinking alcohol by an obviously angry brother that I didn't touch the stuff until he invited me to the pub to celebrate my eighteenth birthday. I took notice of an admired elder brother, whereas a lecture from my father (which would have been delivered with the same passion as my brother put into his spiel) would have fallen on deaf ears.

If you are the parent of a teenager you may be lucky to have a mentor ready to enter your young person's life. Your child might have already forged a relationship with an uncle or aunt, a neighbour or an admired sports coach. You can't exactly relax and take it easy, but it can be a relief to have a trusted ally looking out for your child. If you are not so lucky then it may be that you have to engineer some help. The Big Brother, Big Sister program that matches young adults with young people for weekend and further visits is a successful mentoring program with impressive results, but there are just not enough big brothers and sisters to go around.

It helps for parents to be part of strong social groups that provide opportunities for adults and children to come into meaningful contact with each other. Sports and activities such as cricket, surf lifesaving and guiding bring adults into contact with teenagers through mutual activities.

THE SPECIAL ROLE OF COACHES

Sports coaches and adults involved in youth movements such as guiding and scouting have a very special role to play. Most people initially become involved through their own children. Rather than sit back and watch, they choose to help. There are arguably few more valuable contributions that people can make to the community than to become involved in a hands-on way with children and young people. It is not so much the skills of the particular sport or activity that are of value but the place that the people involved play in kids' lives. For years I have coached kids' sports with varying degrees of success. I have coached kids in sports where my skill knowledge has been limited to say the least. But it is not the skills that I pass on that are the real value but the fact that I might have spent an hour or two a week in their company and that maybe in that time something of myself just might have rubbed off.

Recently I spoke at a scout leaders' conference about dealing with difficult kids. The leaders joined the organisation presumably because they believed in its ideals and wanted to pass something on to the next generation. Many of the leaders were frustrated because many of the children in their packs and troops showed little interest in learning – for many children the social aspects took precedence. The leaders agreed that for a significant proportion of the boys and girls in their packs they were a rare stable adult in their lives, so they filled an important need for these kids. The legacy they left was far greater, but less obvious, than the ability to tie knots or erect tents.

KIDS AS RESOURCES

One of the characteristics of healthy communities is that young people have the chance to be involved in constructive activities. One American study showed that fifty-five per cent of kids in healthy communities were actively involved in sports, clubs, music and other community-sponsored activities whereas in communities classified as high-risk only thirty-nine per cent of young people were involved in these activities.

Several factors are at work when kids become involved within their local communities. It is more than just the notion that by keeping kids busy they are less likely to be involved in anti-social behaviours, although this is a factor. Community activities provide young people with the opportunity to set their own goals and experience the accomplishment of reaching them rather than having goals set for them. It is often through community involvement that young people have their first opportunity to contribute to the lives of others – to be a resource rather than a problem. When young people coach, teach or help others, they learn valuable personal leadership skills, but many experience for the first time being a useful person who can contribute positively to the lives of others. Importantly, community perceptions of young people, which are usually negative, change when they are given the chance to be resources.

IT'S NOT MY PROBLEM

It is easy to become overwhelmed with the enormity of young people's problems, throw your hands up in the air and say that the government must do something or add the problems to the growing list of social issues for schools to address. When problems and communities become too large it is natural to look for someone 'out there' to fix it up. Community begins at home. It is in small ways that people can actively enter the lives of young people and make a difference.

There are examples everywhere of good citizenship and leadership shown by adults towards young people. For instance, a small businessperson who was tired of having trees ripped out of his nursery by young adolescents with nothing better to do began a youth group to keep them off the streets in a meaningful way. It took considerable effort and guile to cajole others in the community into believing that it would be in their long term best interests to explore positive options to keep young people out of trouble. Another example is the basketball coach in her fifties who delights in forming an under-twelve boys basketball team and taking that same team through to under-twenty-one level so she can create something special with a group. She takes more than a personal interest in each and everyone's well-being. Then there is the family who for years have brought a young boy growing up in difficult circumstances into their home every second weekend just to help out and give him a bit of love and support. No money changes hands and he gives them some grief when he acts out but they are contributing in no small way to the community.

There are simple but heroic stories such as these everywhere that serve as a reminder that community starts and finishes with you, the individual. If we are to have positive, resilient children we need to surround them with adults who are leaders and who take a positive approach to all aspects of their lives. That's not easy, but, as I said at the start of this book, raising kids is not for wimps.

REFERENCES

Acland, Jeannette 1998, *Whole Parish Parenting*, Anglican Diocese of Melbourne, Melbourne.

Balson, Maurice 1981, *Becoming Better Parents*, ACER, Melbourne.

Burns, E. Timothy 1996, *From Risk to Resilience*, Marco Polo, Dallas.

Courtenay, Bryce 1993, *April Fool's Day*, William Heinemann, Australia.

Covey, Steven R. 1990, *The Seven Habits of Highly Effective People*, The Business Library, Melbourne.

Dreikurs, Rudolf 1987, *Children: The Challenge*, E.P. Dutton, New York.

Goleman, Daniel 1995, *Emotional Intelligence*, Bantam, New York.

Gottman, John 1997, *The Heart of Parenting*, Bloomsbury, London.

Grose, Michael 1997, 'Parenting Ideas' (blackline masters), ACER, Melbourne.

—1998, 'Parenting Ideas 2' (blackline masters), ACER, Melbourne.

Munson, Pat 1991, 'Winning Teachers/Teaching Winners'.

Robbins, Anthony 1997, *Unlimited Power*, Fireside, New York.

Seligman, Martin 1995, *The Optimistic Child*, Random House, Australia.